Coppeen – A Glimpse Of The Past

Coppeen Archaeological Historical and Cultural Society
(CAHCS)

Solas Nua Publications

First published in West Cork Ireland in June 2007 by
SOLAS NUA PUBLICATIONS
Coppeen, Enniskeane, County Cork, Ireland

Cover design by Shane & Colum Cronin.
All images copyright © Colum Cronin

Copyright © Coppeen Archaeological, Historical and Cultural Society 2007
www.coppeenheritage.com

Edited by Colum Cronin

ISBN: 978-0-9556114-0-7

Printed in Ireland by Inspire Design and Print, Skibbereen Co. Cork

This book is dedicated to the memory of

John Sheehan,
Bishopstown, and formerly of Kilmurry.
DIED 31st MAY 2006

John guiding CAHCS on a tour of Kilcrea Abbey, in July 2005

John's warmth of character, generosity of spirit and vast knowledge of
local history has touched and inspired many of us who aspire to walk a
similar path.

Ar dheis lámh Dé go raibh a anam dhílis

Contents

Foreword

Welcome to the initial historical publication of the Coppeen Archaeological Historical and Cultural Society (CAHCS) We hope you enjoy this journey through time and recall the people and events, customs and practices which helped shape our area and make us into the community we are today.

The past is important, and from it we have forged a unique identity and a way of life which grounds and informs us in all aspects of our daily lives. Without an appreciation of our local historical past we are devoid of identity and culturally deprived. Local history is a window to our past and the essence of who we are now. To those who have contributed to this collection of articles we offer our sincere thanks and hope that you the reader will enjoy this glimpse of our past.

This publication offers an eclectic mix of facts, anecdotes and recollections where the characters and events portrayed were once as real as you and I. Tomorrow we will be shadows and memories as they are now. Enjoy!

Colum Cronin
(Chairman, CAHCS)

Introduction

The inaugural meeting of CAHS (Coppeen Archaeological and Historical Society) was held in An Caipín bar Coppeen on February 14th 2004. On Monday March 1st, the first meeting was held with the ratification of the new society. The name was later broadened to CAHCS (Coppeen Archaeological Historical and Cultural Society). Our Mission Statement is *'to research, restore and preserve all aspects of our archaeological, historical and cultural heritage, and foster an appreciation of same, near and far'*.

The Current Committee:
President: Ned Barrett
Chairman: Colum Cronin
Secretary: Gerard Lordan
Treasurer: Nuala Lordan

Our area is very rich in archaeological terms, and we believe these sites should be highlighted, preserved and in some cases restored, with appropriate signage provided. We have numerous examples of ringforts, stone circles, megalithic tombs, galáns, fullacht fiadh, southerrains, anomalous stone groups, stone rows, stone pairs, rock art, boulder burials, early ecclesiastical remains, fonts and burial grounds.

Each month, the society holds a meeting, (usually on the first Wednesday) with many guest speakers invited in to talk on their specialist subject. Lectures in the past have covered topics such as Ringforts, Stone Circles, The Healing Power of Local Plants, Kilcrea Abbey, The Creameries, Sam Maguire, The West Cork Railway, Lighthouses, Holy Wells, The Michael Collins Story, Shipwrecks and the Coppeen Gold Hoard. When European Heritage Week comes around (August/September of each year), the society usually hosts an event to widen peoples knowledge of our local heritage. In the past, we have held a talk at Kinneigh Round Tower and Gurranareigh Famine Monument, as well as having a Scoriocht in Barrett's Bar, Coppeen, which was a tremendous success. In the past, we have also held outings for members to places such as Kilcrea Abbey. Last year, the society travelled to Cobh, and were given a guided tour of the Old Church Cemetery by Tim Cadogan, followed by a slide show on Cobh. We were then left to wander around the picturesque town, before heading to the

Commodore Hotel for a much enjoyed meal.

Since our formation, we have held a number of events in the locality which have become annual occurrences, such as our very successful Craft Fair, which displays all local crafts and skills, and our fund raising Table Quiz which is always an enjoyable event.

On 31st August 2005, CAHCS launched its website, coppeenheritage.com, and the Coppeen Waymarked Walks System. This was a momentous occasion for the society. The official launch was performed by Ian Dempsey M.D. of West Cork Leader, from whom we received funding for the website. The website gave us a presence on a world wide scale, and enabled us to share our heritage and local information with people all around the globe. The Waymarked Walks System has proven to be a great success, with the society holding regular walks on these picturesque routes, along with people from outside the area. (Walks information and maps available in An Caipín, or check our website)

Much more is planned by the society for the future. A major survey was recently carried out on Kinneigh Graveyard and it is hoped that conservation, restoration and documentation work will soon begin. All events held by the society are advertised locally, or on our website, and everybody is most welcome to join. With just under 30 members at present, newcomers are always welcome and with new projects always in the pipeline, there is always something to keep us busy!

CAHCS is a VOLUNTARY non-commercial group.

Coppeen Archaeological Historical & Cultural Society
Annual General Meeting 2nd March 2005

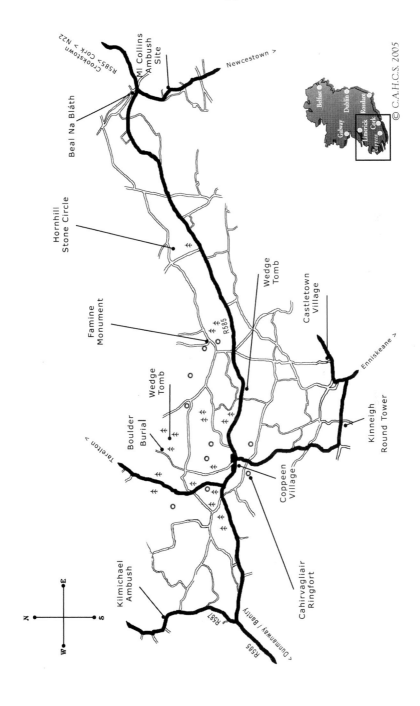

Ml Collins Ambush Site

Beal Na Bláth

Crookstown > Cork > N22
R585>

Newcestown >

© C.A.H.C.S. 2005

Belfast
Dublin
Galway
Rosslare
Limerick
Cork
Coppeen

Hornhill Stone Circle

Wedge Tomb

Castletown Village

Enniskeane >

Famine Monument

R585

Wedge Tomb

Kinneigh Round Tower

Tarelton >

Boulder Burial

Coppeen Village

Kilmichael Ambush

Cahirvagliair Ringfort

R587

R585

< Dunmanway / Bantry

N
E
S
W

Coppeen Village – from 1840 to 2007

The Ordinance Survey map of 1840 shows no trace of a building in the general area of where today's village of Coppeen is situated. This same map shows a cluster of buildings on both sides of the road at the bottom of the hill beyond (North West of) Finbarr O'Driscoll's farmyard. Evidence suggests that a bakery business operated from here. The old school which was located near the bridge, at the far side of the river, was opened on 29th October 1860. Between 1850 and 1880 the house which later became the post office was built. It seems that the very first public house (or shebeen) in Coppeen (owned by Murphy's Sliabhowen) operated here. A dwelling house was built across the road (eastern side) where Patrick (Pake) Murphy resided and operated a general merchant store from about 1890. (Later, this was used as a practice hall for the Coppeen Fife and Drum Band, and later again, was part of the mill store.)

In 1919, Murphys employed Jer Hourihan and Coakleys from Dunmanway to build a new house and shop across the road (later to be McCarthys) and operated a highly successful business there for almost three decades. They installed an oil engine to drive a grain roller and grinder. They had two trucks on the road, along with at least two horse and carts, carrying out the business of collecting eggs and butter, and delivering foodstuffs. When Patrick died on 14th November 1934, his brother John, who had a shop at Moneycrohy Cross, then took over the running of the business. In 1947 John sold the business and bought a local farm. (He subsequently sold this farm to John Hennessy, and bought the 'Muskerry Bar' in Templemartin) Ted McCarthy, and his wife Patricia, were the new owners of the Coppeen property, and they ran a successful general merchant and farm feeds business until the early 1980s when they retired, selling the property to the Barrett family.

Towards the end of the 19th century a public house was erected on the location of Barretts old bar, which stood where the present 'Village Store' now stands. The first registered owner was John Murphy, who married Kate Ryan. Their son Denis Murphy (known as 'Dennie the Publican') next

James Barrett 1890 - 1965   *Patrick Murphy*

took charge. He married Hannah Holland and they had three children, a boy and two girls. Their mother Hannah died at a young age and her sister Mrs Foran took the children into care in Cork. The boy died aged 12. One sister joined the Poor Clare Nuns, and died in France in 1926, and the other sister Helena Henrietta was the heir to the Coppeen business. In the meantime, their father Dennie married Kate Crowley from Aherlick, but he died shortly afterwards, a victim of the 'Black 'Flu', and his wife Kate ran the business until she died in 1916. Then her brother Denis Crowley took charge, followed by Tommy Crowley, who died, followed by his sister Maggie who married James Lynch. They left the business in 1921 and went to live in a cottage west of Coppeen. (When Maggie died, James emigrated to the USA.)

Helena Henrietta Murphy assumed ownership of the business in 1921 when she became of age, and later that year she married James Barrett. At this time, their twin businesses ran side by side in the same room, with the bar counter on one side, and the grocery shop counter on the opposite side. An animal feeds store operated out of a compact loft in the western end of that same building. Underneath the loft was a stall for two cows and a stable for a horse. Just west of this building was a piggery. In 1929 Jamie Crowley was contracted to build an extension across the back of the building to act as a separate shop. In 1931, having finished the building of the new national school, building contractors Dennehys of Belgooly undertook a refurbishment of Barrett's bar, re-locating the counter and improving the

1907 receipt from Murphy's shop (now Barretts)

Mrs McCarthy in her grocery shop (1983)
(An Caipín Bar now stands here)

general layout. In 1931 a new animal feed store was built. It took Helena and James until 1936 to clear the debts which they had inherited from previous owners. Then in 1937, cruelly, in her 38th year, Helena died of peritonitis, leaving James to rear a young family and run a growing business. A new 2 ton V8 truck was bought in 1937.

In 1939, a Dan Jones from Cork was employed to design and erect a hydro-electric generating system, which supplied electric power for Barrett's business and domestic lighting needs during those war years and indeed, beyond. The business continued thus until 1955 when the rural electrification scheme brought about many positive changes. While he had been working in the business from a young age, Ned Barrett had now taken on a more senior role in running the business, having been carefully groomed for this position by his father. A new Christy Norris grain grinder was installed, with a ½ ton mixer – later upgraded to 2 tons capacity. This facility meant that rations could be formulated; leading to a rapid expansion of the farm feeds supply business. In 1964, a section of the old house was demolished, and a new two-storey flat-roofed building was erected by

Castletown - Kinneigh Harriers 1956
Assembled on main road in front of Coppeen Old Post-Office, with McCarthy's shop, store & petrol pumps in background

Coppeen village in the mid 1970s
- note Mobile Bank vehicle

Tim and Jerry Carroll of Johnstown, which included a modern bar with living quarters overhead. On the 3rd May 1965 James Barrett died aged 75 years. Many older people still speak of his many attributes. While his astute business sense was obvious, his understanding, sensitivity and kindness shown towards countless customers, particularly during those war years and their aftermath will never be forgotten.

In 1969, the course of the road was changed, and a by-pass was created to the south of the village This had profound effects on the village of Coppeen, particularly in terms of easing the traffic flow at the doorsteps of both Barrett's and McCarthy's business premises. Around this time, with a need to expand his milling facilities, Ned Barrett purchased a section of property from Feenie O'Driscoll, which was directly across the road from the existing shop and mill. 1975 saw the completion of a modern state-of-the-art mill and ration making facility on the newly acquired site. This facility, manned by a large workforce, along with a large fleet of trucks ushered the 'James Barrett & Sons' business successfully into the 21st Century. Ned purchased McCarthys premises in the early 1980s, and the bar was transferred to the downstairs section of the building for a short period. Then this building was demolished, and a new building incorporating a lounge / bar, meeting room, kitchen and accommodation quarters was built. This beautiful new facility named 'An Caipín' was officially opened in August 1989.

The title of the business ignores one vital ingredient of the Barrett empire over the years; the women family members. From when she took over the fledgling debt ridden business in 1921, Helena Murphy / Barrett was a strong driving force behind the business until her untimely death in 1937. Along with Ned, the other siblings, boys and girls alike, were all expected to share in the work. Then Ned married Theresa Murphy, who, along with becoming an integral part of the business administration, added her own style and panache to the company. Like the generation before them, the girls in the family partook in the work whenever they were needed. Etta was in charge of the grocery shop and bar for some years, and was sorely missed by many of her customers when she decided to leave Coppeen to be a full-time mother to her young family. Therése then became the proprietor of 'An Caipín' bar, where she and her husband Conor Bourke now run a highly successful public house. John continues the milling and farm supply business, while Jim has diversified, forming a ready-mix concrete company. And so the James Barrett & Sons business continues to prosper. The lives and actions of the Murphy, Barrett and McCarthy families have been woven into the social fabric of our society, without which Coppeen and its surrounding districts would have been a much poorer place.

Several generations of the O'Driscoll family have been associated with the old post office building. Records show that Florence O'Driscoll (born 29th July 1855) became the first postmaster in Coppeen on 11th April 1886. The scene of Francis standing at the door, keeping a watchful eye on the happenings of the village, is an abiding memory of many people. This quaint and distinctive building, along with the western section of Barrett's shop, are in 2007, the last remnants of that bygone era. Many of the older generation speak fondly of Crosses' Forge which was located a short distance east of the village. Seven generations of smiths practiced their trade here. In the course of carrying out this book research project, this writer has noticed that, over the past century, the names of O'Driscoll, Barrett and Cross appear regularly and often collectively, suggesting that these families were intrinsically involved in community affairs down through the years.

In the early 1980s Cork County Council started a housing project located just west of the old post office. Today, six houses stand here, as the evolution of Coppeen village continues, and meets the challenges and demands of new generations.

FOOTNOTE: Remember, Coppeen Village is not located in Coppeen! It is in Munigave West. The border between Munigave and Coppeen townlands is defined by the river which flows at the far (southern) side of the main road. Coppeen Cross is located at the southern side of the school. The name Coppeen or 'Cappeen' as it is named in older maps is defined thus by Bruno O'Donoghue (1986 p. 81): 'Cappeen: Caipchin – little wood clearance, crest of hill'.

Cahirvagliair Ring Fort

Introduction

Coppeen and its surrounding areas hold a wealth of historical sites, monuments, information, and unique archaeological features. The fort of Cahirvagliair is one of the most notable of these unique sites. It is a bivallate ringfort and was one of the chief residences of the Cineál Laoighaire. It has been suggested that the name comes from the Fort of the Son of Laoighaire 'Cathair Mhac Laoighaire'. The fort has also been connected through local folklore to one of Ireland's best known historical figures, Brian Boru. It is believed that Brian was held hostage here when he was a young boy between the ages of 8 and 16 years. It has been suggested that because of its size and the stonework in the entrance, that Cahirvagliair must have been built by someone of great importance and it is believed by many to have been a royal residence.

Detail

Cahirvagliair Fort was taken into state care in 1915, but despite this, the fort is in very poor condition. The fosses and ditches which were restored in 1983 and '84 are now in parts, almost non-existent after being flattened. The internal diameter is 42 metres and the overall diameter is 75 metres.

The style of masonry in the entrance can be compared with that found in early masonry churches except that no mortar was used. Features in common include the use of large dressed stones roughly coursed, the use of large thin stones placed on edge to give the impression of massiveness, and the plinth at the base of the wall. It was from these common features that archaeologists estimated the time period in which the fort was built to be within a century or two of AD 1000. The arrangement of the banks and ditches suggest that the projecting entrance was an original feature of the fort, supporting this estimation. Also, during the excavation, no evidence of earlier entrances was found. As there is no causeway across the outer ditch leading to the entrance, it was thought that there may have been a wooden bridge there originally.

Cahirvagliair Ringfort in foreground, with Coppeen village
© Colum Cronin 2006

According to local tradition, when the old school at Coppeen was being built, the contractor robbed stones from the entrance to Cahirvagliair Fort. According to the story, they only stopped when a 'foxy' haired woman appeared at the entrance and frightened them off.

The entrance is of course the main attraction and this statement was made about the site in *The Journal of Irish Archaeology*: 'It is difficult to find a parallel for this entrance in an earthen ringfort but lintelled entrances do occur in stone forts. Generally these entrances are different from Cahirvagliair in that the gate would not be part of a projecting structure, the stones would not normally be dressed and the passage would not be as long.'

The fort has been excavated twice: firstly by antiquarian Windele in June of 1856. In his account of his first visit to the fort in 1840, he stated, 'But the most striking object is the covered passage at the east side, and near the

© Colum Cronin 2004

cairn, formed of two sidewalls, and covered over with large transverse stones.' He also stated, 'The whole of this very interesting monument is worthy of being diligently explored, its cave and its cairn opened and the gateway entrance, the covered way put in repair. There are few monuments like it in the Country.'

In his excavation in 1843, Windele was aided by Fr. Dan O'Sullivan P.P. The fort was, at this time, owned by a Mr. Hungerford. It was noted that the entrance was in very bad repair, with the exterior having received much injury and the outer covering stone fallen. Some of the lintels lining the roof of the entrance were also fallen.

The owner, Mr. Hungerford, had found what he described as caves two years previously. These were formed from earth and in some chambers, the roof was formed by flagstones. A boy, it was said, could stand or sit in some, and in others could creep on all fours. The only items found in the caves were some animal and human bones.

Following Windele's, there was one other excavation which took place at the site; this one in April of 1984 under the direction of Conleth Manning. It was during this time that a more detailed excavation and restoration took place. The entrance was then restored beautifully, and contained most of the original stone work. (Two lintels were missing from the original roof of the entrance).

Excavation of the site turned up very few artefacts, including several stone artefacts, a piece of iron slag, a scrap of iron and some animal bones. One of the stone artefacts found was an 'oblong mudstone pebble' with a groove cut around it closer to one end than the other. Another was an egg shaped pebble which had a black coating in places and appeared to have been subjected to heat. Also found was a portion of a perforated disc of sandstone with concentric grooves on one face.

An important hoard of late Bronze Age gold ornaments was found in the last century in 'a fort in Coppeen'. As there are two ringforts in the townland of Coppeen East and one in Coppeen West, it is difficult to determine which ringfort was the one in question. In 2006 a substantial fence was erected around the fort by the OPW.

A private survey carried out by the Ballineen Enniskeane Area Heritage Group recorded that there is an ever increasing number of visitors, especially European Students of Archaeology, travelling long distances to visit this site.

The Pig – From Conception to Consumption

Today's generation of young people will never witness for themselves the central role which the pig played in rural communities across the country in the past. From the conception of a litter of Bonham's right through to the serving of a piece of steaming bacon and cabbage at the kitchen table the image of community and neighbourly friendships are never far away. In a world of fast moving lives and vacuum packed bacon here is a reminder of how times have changed in the lifecycle of the pig!

In times past pigs were organic and free range, only brought in at night to sleep and be fed. The pigs were housed in a piggery or piggery yard. A household might have had between 2 and 4 sows, depending on the housing that was available.

The Sow in Young

A sow would have produced two litters of bonhams a year. From the time of conception to the time of birth took 16 weeks. A male pig, called a boar, was only kept by a few households in an area, unlike the sow. The sow would either be walked to the place where the boar was kept to breed, or taken by horse and crib. The Department of Agriculture provided a boar for some, and these pigs were known as the Department Pig. The names of those who received a Department Pig were contained in a book which was freely available and which children were fascinated by. An application could be made to the Department if a boar was required.

The Sow Farrowing

When the sow began to farrow she was brought into the kitchen and put on a bed of hay. The furniture was re-arranged or taken outside to make enough room for the accommodation of the sow within the kitchen. A stick would have been placed along the wall in some areas to keep the sow from lying up against it, and killing her bonhams as a result.

A member of the household (or sometimes two) stayed up at night to try and avoid accidents to the bonhams after they were born. The sow would also have to be taken out during the night in order to attend to the call of nature! If more than one person stayed up there was conversation, if not the lone minder might read or fall asleep.

The new family was kept in the dwelling house for a couple weeks after farrowing, so they had access to the heat of the open fire. The usual time was a week or a fortnight, but in cold weather they would have been inside for 3 weeks. The only time the sow was taken outside of the house was to be fed.

It was not unusual to have two sows in the house at the same time. One may have been about to farrow, and the second may have already had her litter of bonhams. A table was placed between the sows if they did end up in the house at the same time.

Once the sow and bonhams were taken out of the house for good the floor was scrubbed clean, and the squeals from the little bonhams were not missed! The freedom of having the house back was not lost on the human inhabitants.

With modernisation came the farrowing crate, into which the sow would be put before farrowing. This helped prevent the sow killing the bonhams, which was previously a worry.

The Pig at the Fair

Pigs to be sold at the fair would have been between 12 and 14 weeks old, the first seven weeks of which were spent with their mother. Each farmer would have kept a couple of pigs from the litter to fatten for themselves. The extra bonhams were sold at fairs. The fairs in this area were held in Macroom, Ballineen and Dunmanway, and took place monthly. The bonhams would have been taken to the Fair in a horse and crib.

The people who bought pigs at the Fair would not have had any sow of their own, and could buy a number of litters from different farmers. These litters were then fattened before being sent to factories in Ballincollig (Farmer's Union) and Cork (Lunhams, Murphy Evergreens, Dennys).

The Fairs died out when the marts came on-stream.

Killing the Pig

The pig was killed outside, on a table or footpath. A specific person killed the pig, and this person would often do it for a number of neighbours. It was known in the locality when a pig was to be killed, and neighbouring men would gather for the killing. Three or four men held the pig and a

rope was used to tie him down. A designated knife was used to kill the pig and a bucket was held underneath it to gather the pig's blood. The pig's body was scalded with boiling water while still warm and shaven with a butcher's knife. Then the intestines were removed and some kept. Following this the pig's legs were tied and he was hung from the ceiling, with the head facing the floor, to solidify the meat and give it a good quality.

The Pig for Food

The pig was cut up into manageable pieces after the pig had been hanging for about 24 hours. The pieces were salted, using large quantities of salt, on a table and put into a wooden barrel, made by a cooper. When all the meat was packed in more salt was poured on top of it and a bag was placed over it. A big stone was put over this to keep down the weight. The salt turned to pickle in the sealed barrel and the meat became cured to what we know as bacon after six to seven weeks. The bacon was then taken out after this time and hung from the ceiling joists. The pickle was then thrown away. Some people dried out the tub and put the meat back into the tub to be stored, after it had dripped and was dry. The meat was now cured and ready to eat as bacon from here on.

The blood gathered at the killing of the pig was used to make puddings. The innards were also used for black puddings, and for sausages in some areas. The intestines were used to hold the sausage ingredients together. A blood cake, described as 'beautiful', was made from the gathered blood, onions, pepper and salt, spices and some fat.

A custom of giving a piece of the cured meat to neighbours when a pig was killed was common, and when the next neighbour killed a pig they returned the custom. And when the meat was gone and the next pig was ready to be killed the cycle started again…

St. Bartholomew's Church, Kinneigh

2006 marked the 150th anniversary of the dedication of the church of St Bartholomew in Kinneigh which took place on August 27th 1856. The rector Rev. Judith Hubbard-Jones arranged a 'quiet act of Evening Prayer' on Sunday 27th August 2006. Then a commemoration service was held on Sunday 8th October, when a capacity crowd enjoyed an evening of prayer, a play reading performance, plainchant hymns and traditional hymns to compliment an appropriate rededication ceremony.

According to the *Annals of Cork*, the monastery at Kinneigh was founded by St. Mocholmóg (St Coleman) in the year AD 619. It was situated about half a mile west of the present site of the Round Tower. Very little is known of its history, and none of the buildings remain. The monastery grounds is said to have covered 16 acres. A rock outcrop known as 'The Castle Rock' was within the monastery grounds as was an old cemetery and another part of the grounds was known as the 'Abhalgort' or Orchard.

In AD 916 the Danes plundered and destroyed Kinneigh Monastery. The survivors then moved east to Sleenoge where they established a new monastery, and later a round tower. This monastery became a Cathedral of a diocese consisting of seven, maybe eight parishes. This diocese was united to the Cork diocese at the Synod of Kells in 1152. It is widely believed that the round tower was built around 1014, though some are of the opinion that it may have been approximately 100 years later. While information is sparse on the period, it appears that the original church fell into disrepair during the late 1600s, just after the reformation. In 1794 a new church was built just south of where the first church stood.

Donald Wood writes: 'A new church, dedicated as Christ Church, was built in the early 1790s near the base of the old ruined church. The building was financed by a grant from the Commission of First Fruits and cost the sum of 461 pounds ten shillings and nine pence farthing. The 1837 Ordnance Survey map shows this church, located near the middle of the old graveyard. A lithograph print which dates from the early 1800s of the Round Tower and church appears on Tony Brehony's book on the *History*

*Rev. Judith Hubbard-Jones cutting a celebratory cake at the
150th Commemoration Ceremonies at St. Bartholomews Church,
watched by David Bourne*

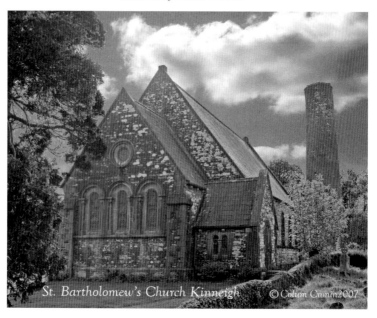

of West Cork. The church is shown with a low tower and conical spire, very much how it is described in Lewis's *Topographical Dictionary* of 1837. The old glebe house is shown beside the round tower. By the end of the 20th century this building had become ruined but most of the structure still stood. Griffith's surveyors recorded the dimensions of the church in 1847. The tower and spire were recorded as 40 feet 9 inches high on a base of 14 feet by 13. The church was 48 feet long, 36 feet wide and 15 feet 6 inches high.'

Christ Church had a curiously short life of just 62 years before a new one (the present St Bartholomew's) was built. The stones from Christ Church were used to build the wall around the new church and southern grave-yard.

In conclusion, it appears that St Bartholomew's is the third church to exist in this area. The previous two stood in the middle of the present old graveyard. What if those stones could talk?!

Flax Linen

People started growing flax in the Newcestown area in about 1945. It was a labour intensive crop but a very profitable one if done well. It could yield up to £100 per acre. Flax spent about 100 days in the ground. It was planted using an implement called the fiddle. There were beautiful blue flowers which only lasted a few days. It looked like an acre of bright blue sky in the field. It would be better if no rain fell for a few days after the flowers arrived. Heavy rain could lodge the flax. The flax would benefit from dry weather before pulling.

Things had to be well organised for the day of the harvesting as everything had to be completed in one day. The men who worked at the flax needed to be young and able bodied. Flax had to be pulled by hand and put in sheaves to be bound with binder twine. There were about four men pulling. Machines were later used. It was then drawn by horse and cart to the pond. Usually about twenty horse loads. Streams had to be damned as there could be no water in the pond when the flax was put in. It had to be laid properly in the pond and its roots should not be damaged. Then, fairly big stones had to be put on top because it would float. The water was then allowed in. It should be fresh water and when the pond was full there couldn't be any leaks. The pond was then by passed by the stream. Men had to stand on the stones to keep the flax down until it was fully wet. It was left in the pond for about ten days and then the stones taken out.

Once drawn to the field the sheaves were opened and spread out for about four to five days depending on the weather. It was then drawn to the factory. At this stage, after its time spread out in the field twenty loads were reduced to about four which looked like blonde hair (flaxen hair). The water in the pond was poison for animals and plants so it had to be disposed of carefully.

Water Divining

The ability to water divine is derived from an electrical source within the human body. Some have more than others. The smaller the amount the better for the human heart. People with a large amount of electricity in the body can do divining and those with very little can not do it

Water divining puts a strain on the heart and you do not feel well after doing the job. The instrument usually used is a 'Y' shaped piece of hazel or sally tree of even strength on both sides called a *gabhlóg* (pronounced 'gow-logue'). A gabhlóg can also be made from a bronze welding rod, or the wire of a clothes hanger. The water diviner holds the gabhlóg in his hands with his fists faced up and walks along in one direction until he found a spring or underground stream. When he was comes near the spring the gabhlóg would begin to turn down to the ground and when he comes directly over the spring it points straight down in his hands, regardless of how he tries to hold it. If he tried to hold it over a very strong spring the wood gabhlóg would break with the pressure and the bronze or wire gabhlóg would bend.

When the diviner goes past the spring, the gabhlóg would face back between his legs and pressure would hold on until you went a certain distance past the spring. If you measure from that point, back to the point where the gabhlóg pointed straight down over the spring, that would be a rough estimate of the depth of the spring.

Water diviners usually look for a point where two springs are crossing. One is always deeper than the other, so if you can catch both springs you will have a better supply of water. In a drilled well if a lot of water is pumped out you would hear the water from the top spring running down the side of the bore hole. When this is heard, you know that you have a powerful supply of water.

Nowadays, people draining wet land especially at the southern side of a hill often get a water diviner to mark the springs, and if drains are made directly in those markers you will end up with a very successful job.

Diving is also used to find other minerals such as copper, zinc, iron and sometimes even humans. If you hold something in your hand such as cap, sock or part of under clothing that was in contact with the body being sought, the gabhlóg would move when the diviner comes over the body. Another thing the diviner could tell is, if a male or female sat on a chair, using a needle with a wooden thread in it. If it moves in a circle it was a male and if it moved from left to right it was a female who last sat on the chair. If there are electric cables buried under ground and if the diviner holds a bit of copper cable in his hand, when he comes over the cable it will point down.

Noted Diviners:

Johnny Chambers, Ballinaure   Denis O Donovan, Ardcahan
Tim Joe Hurley, Lissarourke   'OD' O'Donovan, Bengour
Donal O Brien, Clashbredane   Mr. Kiely, Ballinhassig

Using a gabhlóg

Stone Circles

Stone Circles are more often than not associated with the Stone Age but they are in fact Bronze Age monuments. The Bronze Age began about 2000 BC in Ireland. Most Stone Circles are small with only five or seven uprights and another large stone positioned flat on the ground outside the circle. Some are very large such as the imposing stone circles at Drombeg, Co. Cork. However, Drombeg is an exception as it is dated to somewhere between 153 BC and AD 127, the Iron Age. Irish stone circles are mostly more charming than impressive. There is also a certain enigma attached to them even to this very day, as their specific function is unknown. The stone circle in Drombeg certainly seems to have been used as a calendar to ascertain the shortest day of the year. Most are aligned with the setting sun. Astronomy aside, they may simply have been temples, a dedication to the sun god. A number of stone circles marked the site of a burial. While stone circles are a delight to the eye, one must remember that looks can be deceptive. Not only does Drombeg function in telling the time, it also marks a burial as a cremated body was found in the centre of the circle when it was excavated. This suggests that stone circles played a crucial part in the lives of the Bronze Age people as they fused time and death together as one. One has to recognise that these stone circles helped the primitive people to indicate a change and an end in the seasons that was about to occur.

There are six stone circles in the Coppeen and surrounding area. It is a rare archaeological occurrence to have six stone circles within a 2-mile radius. This may have something to do with the Bride River, which flows through Beal na Bláth. The Bride River has a sacred significance as it derived its name from the old pagan goddess – Brigit/Bridget. She symbolised fertility.

In this area, one comes across two types; composed of five stones, or multiple stones (contain seven or more stones). No person knows why some stone circles consist of five stones but it is believed they stand for the five elements: water, air, fire, earth, spirit. They are distinguished by the

Knockaneirk Lower Stone Circle   © Colum Cronin 2005

Knockaneirk Upper Stone Circle   © Colum Cronin 2004

Currabeha (southern) Stone Circle   © Colum Cronin 2005

axis stones, which indicate their astronomical orientation. The main axis stone is easy to recognise as it lies on its side and found in the west or southwest side of the stone circle. It is also called the recumbent stone and has a smooth flat surface.

Besides telling the shortest day of the year, it is said that children were sacrificed on the recumbent stone to placate the sun god. One could say that stone circles were religious centres attended by the ancient inhabitants in the surrounding area. They also attracted tribal gatherings to worship their god – the sun. They feared and depended on the sun so much that each tribe elected a high priest to ensure and coax the rising of the sun the next morning, hence children sacrifices.

The Summer and Winter Solstices enhance the many wonders of the stone circle. On the longest day of the year; (the Summer Solstice), the first rays of the sun project between two portal stones, otherwise known as the 'Entrance Stones', and hit the centre of the recumbent stone. On the short-est day of the year, the last rays of the sun cross the threshold between the two portal stones. These two principal events represented the cohabitation of the sun and the earth. One could state that the building of the stone cir-cles was a way of communicating with their sun god. The ancient people's relationship with their sun god was imperative as to guarantee the growth of their crops. The touch of the sun's rays on the recumbent stone was almost like a hand-shake after signing a contract to pledge its part in fertil-izing the soil.

The question still remains of what evidence do we have that suggests stone circles epitomised fertility and that this was the main prayer; if you like, to their sun god to ensure the growth of their crops? Firstly, the shapes of the large stones that complete the stone circle cannot be underestimated. The slender stones on the left hand side of the circle if one is facing the east or towards the 'Entrance Stones' stand for the male sex. On the right hand side of the stone circle, the large stones have rotund silhouettes representing the female sex and the womb. If one took a helicopter ride and viewed a complete stone circle from the sky, it can to some resemble a womb. The union between a man and a woman was considered sacred and magical, so too was the coming together of the sun and the earth, (the projection of the sun's rays through the portal stones or the cervix of the stone circle and hitting the recumbent stone). Both of these unions stood for and produced new life and a new age. This miraculous unity between the sun and the earth and its great similarity to the coming together of a man and woman sexually surrounded the stone circle with a magical aurora. It is palpable from the above information that the stone circle was a versatile tool and the heart of the surrounding communities when it came to comprehending their fundamental beliefs.

The stone circle was also used as an observatory for the astronomers – the elected high priests in antiquity. Carvings of stars on some 'Entrance Stones' of stone circles compel us to believe that they had interest in watching the sky at night. This would also lead us to believe and verify our suspicions of their fear of the sun being immortal. The weather was colder and more settled in ancient times which constituted suitable conditions for solar observation. They could predict by the stars and the constellations at night in lieu of the sun by day what season to expect and to be able to tell accurately when the new season was to occur. Therefore, it would leave the ordinary Joe soap of the ancient people to feel in awe of these supernatural happenings; the Summer and Winter Solstices and the chanting high priests for example. In the early days of the sun cult, great care was taken in building these stone circles. Large stones were selected to complete them. However, when Christianity made its way to our shores by St Patrick in the 5th century, the stone circles were built in a slapdash fashion as the solar cult began to breathe its last breath.

Knockaneirk Lower: This circle is located directly beside the road and is easy to access. This is an incomplete multiple stone circle with seven stones still standing but is otherwise in good state of preservation. The main axis stone, or recumbent stone, is located on the west side of the circle. It is hard to distinguish whether the portal stones are within the seven stones still standing as the presumed portal stones on the east are parallel to another large stone on the west side of the stone circle. The hasty style in which it was erected indicates that it dates around the time the solar religion was diminishing. The missing stones belonging to the stone circle may have been used as building materiel or early Christian fanatics could have eradicated them. This stone circle is likely to be orientated for the Winter Solstice, but it is difficult to confirm as conifers block the view to the west.

Currabeha: This is one such town land that has twin stone circles located not far from each other. An incomplete multiple stone circle that is missing its recumbent stone and which is orientated for the Winter Solstice. An impressive stone circle situated below the first one has a quartz stone positioned in the centre. This is by far the best of the number of stone circles in the Coppeen and the surrounding area. A beaker consisting of ashes was found in the centre of the circle when it was excavated. Hence the name the 'Beaker Burial'. This is a classic stone circle, as the recumbent stone is placed due west. Many of the large stones that make up the stone circle have fallen including one of the portal stones on the left-hand side.

Regrets for Bengour Creamery

By George Godsill

Now there's a spot in County Cork I want you all to know,
It's deserted now for twenty years or more.
Its there we used to gather every morning long ago,
Chatting there outside the creamery store.

In olden days when times were tough and milk was in the can,
The custom was deliver it each day.
To a certain destination where a very efficient man,
Accepted it or sent it the other way.

When the cows were milked and breakfast ate we went to the creamery
store, Where milk was weighed and tested on the spot.
All the farmers joined the queue outside the coal house door,
Through the means of transport varied quite a lot.

The craic was good in Maurice's pub on a Sunday after mass,
Such hunger you could not ask for more.
We were always smiling at the girls as they passed,
As they stepped it out beyond the creamery store.

The forge we knew got modern with a new welding machine,
And sparks and flames came pouring out the door.
Sure all the farmers thought it was the greatest ever seen,
As they passed out beside the creamery store.

Now the pace was far too slow for some as they came to the creamery store,
If you bid them time of day they'd scarcely stop,
While others would take things in their stride and then go down the road,
For a drink and smoke inside in Maurice's shop.

Now years have passed and times have changed since we joined the E.E.C.,
And the winds of change were soon beginning to blow.
Our future may be secure by what we know as the C.A.P,
In Strasburg and in Brussels sure you know.

Yes we were getting modern and the bulk tank soon arrived,
And our beloved store was a meeting place no more.
Sure we were very happy in our innocence long ago,
Chatting there outside the creamery store.
Yes we were very happy in our innocence long ago,
Chatting there outside the creamery store.

The Horse Sprayer

It was in the early 1950s, I decided to buy a horse sprayer, for spraying potatoes. In those years, every farmer had from a quarter of an acre to an acre and a half planted. Horse sprayers were scarce at this time. One sprayer that came around the Tarelton and Coppeen area was from Beal na mBláth. The owner was a Mr. Long and the man in charge was the late Bill Murray, whose family still resides in the Coppeen area.

What a relief it was to see this machine coming into the yard, as opposed to the 'Budget' sprayer, which used to weigh heavily on your back, and used to hold between 2 and 3 gallons. You worked a handle with one hand which pumped the spray and you held the lance with a nozzle in the other hand. The horse sprayer I bought was a Star, as the barrel was going with the length of the sprayer. The Pierce sprayer was another type available, and the barrel on this went across the body, which was dangerous in what was known as a 'Lacka' field. As you were turning at the end of the drill and if the horse turned too fast, with half a barrel of maybe 20 gallons or more, the spray would go to one side and you could get turned over. Each sprayer could hold 40 gallons, and on top of the barrel in the middle, was an opening of about 9 inches squared to put the spray in. A timber funnel with a copper screen to keep leaves and dirt out was used, because the nozzles would block easily. Water was drawn from wells and streams in those days.

The spraying season would start about the 20th of June, and would continue to the first week of August. The sprayer could spray three drills at the time, and each farmer would spray about three times in the season. A foggy evening would always be gladly welcomed by the man in charge, as it always encouraged the blight to hit many a garden. At present, most farmers ring the Met office, and they will get the weather report and so can be ready for the blight. In the field of the garden, the farmer would have a timber barrel, especially for spraying, filled with 40 gallons of water. If he had two barrels to spray he would have two 20-gallon churns of water. The mixture of the spray would be 10lbs of washing soda and 8lbs of bluestone.

The last spray could increase to 12lbs and 10lbs with some people, to make it stronger. Some would also have hot water to melt down the washing soda from big lumps. It would then be taken to the timber barrel and mixed with the bluestone. The owner of the sprayer would have his own bucket, to fill the sprayer.

The farmer would arrange a time with the spraying operator, when to call. On one occasion, I agreed to be there at 11am, but it was after midday when I arrived. He had everything ready at 11am, but the washing soda had gone cold and hard in the bucket, so it needed more hot water. I knew his wife Mary was a wary jade, and he said to her, 'Johnny has come – we need another kettle of hot water.'

She said, 'May the devil take him, and I have a cake in the bastible, that will take ten minutes more, so let him wait.'

At that time there was no electricity, and Jack brought out a small pot of water, he took some of it back in to her, and she said you should have thrown it at him. I had two more farmers that day, who had two and three barrels to spray. I had finished with one of them when it got wet, so I dropped the sprayer and rode the horse home, and rode him back again in the morning. It was 7 miles each way, so I travelled 28 miles in total. The charge per barrel was a half crown, which is about 12.5 cents in today's money and in total I earned 65 cents that day.

One day I sprayed for a farmer, he had two barrels ready, but bygor when he had you started, he was gone. He was stirring the mix in the barrel with a long stick, then filled the bucket and handed it to me on the sprayer. When the rum on the sprayer was full, I straightened my horse over the drills, pushed the lever, and off we went. First spray done, and returned back for the second barrel, I was alone, he was gone. He was the laziest man I met that day, but I don't think he was lazy by night, as he had twelve children.

I remember one year when I had a bad tooth ache, it was a lower tooth, with a big hole in it, and to ease the pain, I would dip my finger in to the sprayer, rub it in to the tooth and it would relieve the pain for a while. I would have to repeat the process, when it started again.

The farmer would get the blue stone and washing soda in the local shop. There it would have been weighed into brown paper bags; all the shops had weighing scales in those times. It normally came to the shop in ten stone bags. You would always be fed by the farmers in those days. Some of them would pay you, when you had the last spraying finished, as money was scarce at that time. More would tell you it would be Christmas when they would have the turkeys sold. 95% of them would pay you. When I was going to school, we were told to pay your lawful debts, and give everyone their own. I wonder if it was taught in all the schools, and the other 5% were suffering from memory loss.

That was my experience of the horse sprayer and hard-earned money.

Kinneigh Round Tower

The typical round tower is a free standing cylindrically shaped building, usually in close proximity to a church and located most likely to its NW or SW side. Distribution fairly evenly covers most of Ireland and even some off shore islands, but two areas, south Munster and the north midlands, have relatively few. County Cork has only 2 extant examples but possibly had up to 6 in the past. In total there are c.64 surviving in Ireland. Round tower windows always ascend clockwise, right to left, and very often four windows mark the upper storey. The latest treatise on round towers, *Ireland's Round Towers*, 2004, by Tadhg O'Keeffe, classifies them using doorways and says doorways give the best indication of tower chronology, though dating them is difficult. In historical sources their destruction was more often recorded than their construction. The first historical reference to a round tower, Slane, Co. Meath, was in AD 950.

Described as a 'curious tower' by O'Keeffe, Kinneigh uniquely has a hexagonal base measuring 18 ft high (fig.2). The drum measures 67ft 3in high and has a 'marked batter'. In the mid-1800s the upper section was added to allow a bell be inserted. It is built of slate laid in reasonably horizontal courses. The stone is 'well squared, especially at the quoins of the base'. All the surviving windows and door are lintelled giving it a plain appearance. The doorway is in the NE face of the base at first floor level, which originally had a flagstone floor. Kinneigh tower is one of eight round towers in Ireland that have all lintelled openings. Kinneigh is incomplete so the possibility exists that the upper storey windows were more elaborate. These 8 towers have a wide distribution across Ireland and stylistically are very simple, and therefore difficult to date. Based on this 'simple' appearance an earlier date for Kinneigh's construction is suggested by O'Keeffe, possibly the tenth or early eleventh century (c.900–c.AD1050). This suggests that the tower could be broadly contemporary with Cahirvagliair ringfort which was dated 'within a century or two of the year AD 1000' (c.800–c.AD1000), which brings us to the function of round towers.

Any discussion of function must take into account the annalistic refer-

© Colum Cronin 2006

ences to round towers. They are frequently referred to as *cloicteach* – bell houses. Death and fatality within towers is another theme, particularly the death of royal or high status persons. The actual morphology of round towers must also tell us something of their function, being as they were singularly unique buildings in their time requiring deep resources, both in terms of money or patronage and craftsmanship. Their use as depositories for relics and/or treasures is another possible function. Looking at

Mr Jerry Falvey, caretaker of Kinneigh Graveyard
for many years

Kinneigh and attempting to tease out its origins and function we must surely take the proximity, both temporally and spatially, of Cahirvagliair bivallate ringfort into consideration. Here we have two high status sites built within possibly 100 years of each other. The distinct possibility exists that Kinneigh was patronised by the household that occupied Cahirvagliair, a household that appears to have had ample resources.

Thomas Edward Wood
– Champion Athlete

In tracking our family tree since the arrival of the first Woods in West Cork in the 17th century we have not come across many who made any significant mark on their times. Almost all were tenant farmers who lived out their lives within a few miles of our birthplace. An exception was the man whose 1896 photograph is shown on the next page.

Thomas Edward Wood was born on the 14th of November 1871. He was the second child of Richard Wood and Mary Ann Kingston of Castlelands. Richard, born 1838, was the second youngest son of William Wood and had married Mary Ann in 1868. William Wood died in 1871 after a long illness and Richard inherited Castlelands. In time a total of ten children were born at Castlelands between 1870 and 1887.

Thomas Edward Wood eventually won the GAA all round Athletic Championship of Ireland in 1895. Michael Cusack had laid the foundations of the GAA only a few years before Thomas Wood entered active competition. The late 19th century was a time of awakening interest in all forms of Irish activities. Until 1922, the GAA, as well as administering traditional Irish ball games, organised Athletics events throughout the country. Within ten years of the formation of the GAA in 1884 its clubs were to be found throughout the island. It is no surprise that a youthful Thomas Wood, though Protestant, would have chosen it as the natural outlet for his talents.

Thomas Edward Wood was an all rounder who is rumoured to have held the Irish Long Jump record briefly, was a competitive hurdler and also threw the Shot – though possibly not the 16 lb one we know today. In 1894 he won the All Ireland Hurdles title. In 1895 he did even better, carrying off titles in running, hurdles and shot putt and, with them, the title of All Round Athletics Champion. In 1896 (coincidentally the year of the first modern Olympic Games) he won the shot putt title again.

He was also a competitive cyclist. An article in an 1890 journal told how he had won an evening cycle race in Cork the previous week. He had

arrived at Ballineen railway station with his bicycle only to be told he had missed the train. Not daunted he pedalled his way to Cork and duly competed in his competition.

After his athletics career was over, Thomas helped his father run his various farms. In 1892 Richard Wood had bought the Paddock – a farm of 127 acres – from his elder brother Edward who had run into financial difficulties. He eventually divided it into two plots. His sons Thomas and Harry inherited these farms. Thomas married Sarah Anne Follis in 1909 and they had one son, Richard Ernest Wood, who was always known as Roy. Initially Thomas and Sarah lived at Mount Lodge just north of Enniskeane. Later they went to live at the Paddock.

Thomas and his son set up a radio repair business at the Paddock which was still operating in the late 1940s. Eventually Thomas retired to a house in the village of Enniskeane leaving Roy to look after the farm on his own. Thomas Edward Wood died in 1945 and is buried in Kinneigh Churchyard. His grave is marked by a Celtic Cross.

Roy was more taken with the radio business than farming and sold the farm in 1952. He bought a house in West London from the proceeds, married Pauline French from Rosscarbery and restarted his electronics business.

Before he died in 1997, Roy visited Croke Park in Dublin and presented his father's ceremonial belt from 1894/5/6 to the GAA museum (see attached photo circa 1986). In the photograph the medals, which were on two separate belts in the 1896 photo, have been moved to one new belt. The medals seem to be one extra large one for the all round title in 1895, two pairs for his wins in shot putt and hurdles and one separate medal for his single running title.

The family of ten children reared at Castlelands by Richard Wood and Mary Ann Kingston has left few traces in West Cork. Five of the children never married and sold their farms as they approached old age. Three emigrated to the UK and married there. Only two (Thomas and Mary) married locally. Between them they produced only three children who had no heirs.

The photo opposite was taken about 1896. Thomas Edward Wood proudly displays his various championship medals mounted on two belts. In the image below his son, Roy and daughter-in-law, are photographed in the 1980s presenting the medals to the GAA museum.

Strange but True

Lost Gold

John Joe had a dream three nights in a row. He was told there was gold buried on his farm; he pinpointed the exact spot in this dream. He thought perhaps it was just a dream but was told there would be a visible sign in the form of a gold pin near where the gold was buried. He found the pin but was still uneasy about digging the spot. In the meantime he told some relation (from his mother's side) living near Timoleague about this dream. Not a very wise decision.

These relations came one night when all was quiet, and found the gold in a skillet pot exactly where John Joe had told them. In the meantime as they were leaving the farm with the gold, poor John Joe asleep in his bed got a feeling of being choked to death. He suffered a stroke and lost his speech. The feeling in the locality was that his ancestors were angry with John Joe for allowing this money, which they had saved for the family, leave the farm. This branch of the family is now extinct.

(The main character's name has been changed to protect family identity.)

Taxi Service

In the fifties, a local man from Gloun provided a taxi service for the young people of the area. This provided a much needed outlet for entertainment. He owned a lorry, and adjusted it by putting seating in the body, and transported from thirty to thirty-five young boys and girls to dances in Inchigeela at a nominal fee.

He parked the lorry about half a mile outside the village and advised his cargo of excited young folk to calmly walk in groups of three or four, at intervals, towards the dance. The Gardaí were in the village and would become suspicious if they saw a group of thirty or forty approaching together and would query where they had come from and the mode of transport provided. This insured that their luxury limo would be available for future dances!

In the summer, he also organised outings to various places of interest in the area, providing tea and buns to his passengers at a price of about 1 shilling and 6 pence per head. These trips were eagerly looked forward to and gave people an opportunity to see places that their parents only dreamed about visiting.

Michael Collins and Beal na mBláth

This Celtic cross monument set on an elevated railed red brick and limestone base marks the spot where General Michael Collins; commander-in-chief of the National Army and chairman of the Provisional Government (Realtas Sealadach) was shot dead during an ambush by anti-Treaty republican irregulars on Tuesday August 22nd 1922. The military convoy escort commanded by General Emmet Dalton comprised a motor-cycle outrider, a Leyland Thomas touring car containing Collins, a Rolls Royce Whippet armoured car (Sliabh na mBan) and a converted Crossley tender containing some twelve soldiers. That fateful morning the convoy had left the Imperial Hotel, Cork, proceeding to Macroom thence to Bandon via Beal na mBláth, next to Clonakilty, Rosscarbery and Skibbereen. Returning it stopped at Rosscarbery and Bandon before being ambushed at Beal na mBláth.

2005 Commemorations at Beal na mBláth   © Colum Cronin 2005

Historians agree that Collins Cork tour had one or more main objectives; to boost the confidence of the populace in the midst of a bitter civil war, to bolster the resolve of the army as the irregulars retreated further west, to sort out misappropriated government funds in a Cork bank and to meet up with anti-Treaty leaders to end hostilities. In this latter regard many believe that the return evening route to the Macroom area was to meet neutral go-between republicans in the parochial house at Lissarda. This would explain the circuitous route through Beal na mBláth since Collins' principal destination was the Imperial Hotel to which he should normally reach via Innishannon or Crossbarry. The ambushing party was part of an anti-Treaty meeting near Beal na mBláth in the morning and when a scout spotted the Collins convoy driving south an ambush was set up on the expectation that he would return later. Believing that the convoy would not return by that route, the engagement was called off with just a few men left taking up a road mine when the convoy suddenly appeared from the Mossgrove direction. Military experts now agree that Collins' countermanding order to stop and fight as against Dalton's 'drive like hell' was militarily unprofessional and a dreadful mistake that cost him his life.

The convoy with its dead leader moved off as dusk fell stopping at Cloughduv Church to seek the last rites at Annesgrove, Aherla, where the mortal wound was washed. Overcoming various obstacles the convoy reached Cork City and Shanakeil Hospital late that night. Local historians believe that two irregulars were also fatal victims of this tragic ambush. Since this awful day theories abound as to who fired the fatal shot. These can be summed up thus; a direct hit from the ambushing party; a ricochet bullet from the ambushing party; an accidental ricochet from the convoy; treachery or shot by a plant of the British secret service in the convoy; and the most bizarre; suicide or para-suicide by Collins from remorse of conscience for signing the Anglo-Irish Treaty and turning arms against his former comrades. Following a huge funeral procession through Cork City, Collins' remains were taken by sea on the funeral ship *Classic* to Dublin. Tens of thousands lined the streets as the horse-drawn gun carriage rumbled on its somber way from the Pro Cathedral to Glasnevin Cemetery where the young founding father of the state was buried with full military honours.

A Portrait of Kilmichael Parish

Kilmichael is a parish partly in the Western Division of the Barony of East Carbery, but chiefly in the Barony of West Muskerry in the County of Cork. It is situated between the towns of Macroom and Dunmanway. It is the second largest parish in the Diocese of Cork, stretching 17 miles in distance. In political terms it is now in the North West Cork Constituency. The population at present is roughly about 1,500, while in the early nineteenth century it was at a very high rate of 6,000. The river Lee forms part of the boundary between Kilmichael and Macroom. At Dromcarra Bridge, where a well is dedicated to St. Michael, the Lee turns northwards to join the Toon River. Further on lies the Gearagh which was a great haunt for poteen making. It was a wilderness of small trees and reeds, part of it was good farmland, but due to the Lee Scheme which took place in the 1950s the land and the houses were flooded. Leaving the Lee we turn to the River Bride. It rises in Renacaheragh and flows in an eastern direction to Crookstown.

The name Kilmichael goes back to the fourteenth century. Legend goes of a monk who cut his hair on Friday. This was forbidden so all the bells rang out as if in protest. The pope heard of this and as a punishment the monk was banished from Rome forever, and was to build a church on where ever he should see a goat grazing on a 'lios'. So after a long journey he arrived at 'Modern Kilmichael'. Going in to a local cottage where he sought refreshments, he heard the phrase being used, 'the goat is grazing on the lios'. Hearing this he recognized journey's end and so built a church and devoted it to St. Michael the Archangel. It was then in 1493 on the 23rd of May, that Matthew O'Mahony became the first parish priest ever in Kilmichael.

It is a parish of many historical places, such as upright stones and forts. The date of their origin is unknown, there is a possibility they date back to the days of the Danes or even as far back as the Druidal days in Ireland. Deshure Fort is a very famous one; it is reckoned there are many underground tunnels linked with smaller forts in different areas. There are many

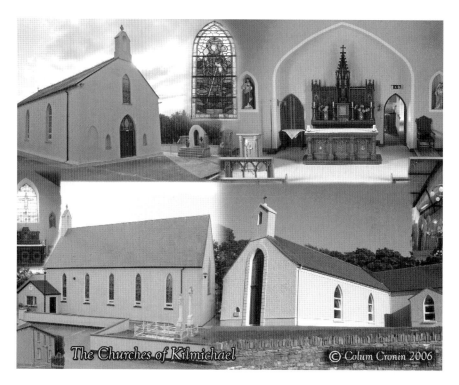

The Churches of Kilmichael
© Colum Cronin 2006

Mass rocks located throughout the parish, one at Cooleclevane, one in Kilnadur and one in Kilnarovanagh. The village of Cooldorrihy was centered between Cooldorrihy House where John Murphy lived and Cooldorrihy Chapel. Outside Murphy's house is a pillar which was used to give notice of eviction in those days. In the village of Cooldorrihy, during the Fenian times, a farm labourer was bayoneted. The priest who went to his assistance was at that time living in the curate's house, which was the home of Lehanes and is now the home of the O'Leary family at Cooldorrihy. That priest was later executed in the place which is now known as the 'Running Kiln', a defunct lime kiln where lime was burned for local farmers and eventually where one of the crossroad platforms was established and is still visible.

Kilmichael is better known for the 'Kilmichael Ambush', where eighteen Auxiliaries from their barracks in Macroom were killed by the famous 'Flying Column' under the command of General Tom Barry. However Kilmichael is far more than just a site of a great victory. It is a parish which is noted far and wide, but particularly in the Diocese of Cork for the very large number of priests and nuns which it has produced, the most recent being Fr. Tony O'Riordan of Cooldorrihy. Among these have been two bishops of Cork and one of Waterford. These were Bishop Cohalan and Bishop Murphy of Cork as well as another Bishop Cohalan of Waterford. Many of these priests played football for Kilmichael including Dr. Michael Murphy, Bishop of Cork, and he also played minor hurling for Cork, the Lucey brothers, Fr. Michael and Fr. Peter, Fr. Dan Bums and Fr. Connie Murphy, the superior of the SMA Fathers in Cork.

Kilmichael has three churches: St. Enda's, Johnstown, St. Michael's, Cooldorrihy, and St. Finbarr's, Toames. There are now three schools, Johnstown, Dromleigh and Tarelton. Dromleigh is one of the oldest schools in Ireland. It was built in 1838. At one time there were eight schools, but some were closed due to the decline in the population. There are a number of public houses, post offices, shops and garages, plus the Dairygold Co-op in Tarelton. At the Northern end of the parish the Ballyclough milk factory was built in the seventies and is now giving employment to a number of people and recently has been taken over by Dairygold. There are two quarries in the parish, one in Cooleclevane and one in Carrigboy.

Kilmichael has been noted for the veterans who fought in the 1914–1918 war, who returned safely and have since died, namely Dan O'Leary of Cooldorrihy, Jeremiah Ring and Thade Foley both of Toames. Another man named John Foley of Knockane, spent some time in the Congo. Jerry Lehane, of Cooldorrihy was one of four people who got a scholarship to Oxford University in the anti-papist times. There were four men who contested the local elections for County Council. They were John Burke of Toames, Jeremiah McCarthy of Aultagh, Christy Kelleher of Inchasine and John O'Callaghan of Cooldaniel, but none succeeded.

In the early fifties a greyhound named 'Ella's Ivy', owned by John J. Riordan of Mountmusic, won the St Ledger at Limerick greyhound track and also qualified for the Lauries at Cork. Willie Buttimer of Deshure, won a stake and cup at the open coursing at Macroom in the sixties with a dog named 'Lee Valley Lad'.

Bowl playing is another important sport in Kilmichael. Some of the bowlers in the county came from the parish, notably the Buckley brothers Tim and Michael, who came from Clashbridane and were able to loft a bowl ninety yards. In later years came the Wood brothers, from Knockane, Walter, Bertie and Tom. Tom was one of the best in Cork at that time. Then in the late sixties and early seventies came another bowler. Jerry Dwyer of

Shanacashel, who has won tournaments all over the county. In the seventies he won a major tournament and travelled to Armagh to play an opponent who won the same competition in Armagh where Jerry was defeated in a great score. In the eighties another young player became famous, this was Pat Thompson of Kilnadur. In 1981 he won the West Cork Championship and then travelled to Armagh to win the All-Ireland. In 1982 he won the West Cork Championship and also the Cork County Championship as well as the All-Ireland in the Under-18s. In 1984 he was awarded the Annual Munster Youth Sports Star award. This was the first time ever that such an honour has been awarded to a Kilmichael man.

As a result of a meeting in Tarelton National School on 27 September 1979, a pitch and putt club was formed and the following officers were elected: Chairman Michael Barry-Murphy, Vice-Chairman Sean Horgan, Secretary Dermot Foley, Treasurer Paddy Foley and PRO Dan O'Keefe. Here numerous volunteers put in many hours of hard work to bring this course in Anahala to the superior level that it is today. Having their own club house and a challenging and intricate course, the club has hosted numerous competitions, over the years, and many of its members have achieved great success on the putting greens all over the county.

Kilmichael produced a Munster Cycling Champion. Dan Harrington, Greenville achieved this in 1924. On that Sunday, he cycled from home to Kinsale, where the Munster Championships were being held. He had his two racing wheels on his back, and once in Kinsale he took off the two common wheels and fitted his racing specials. As champion, as well as his title, he received a gold watch and chain. He changed his wheels again, and cycled the 40 miles home to Tarelton.

Aidan Kelleher, Tarelton became Junior All Ireland Champion in Power lifting in 1984 in Waterford. To keep fit was the main reason he started this sport, working in his own home made gym, he made a name for himself in a very short while. Shortly afterwards another man also took a keen interest in this sport. He also built his own gym, then coached and trained some local lads. Oliver Forde from Renacaheragh, now living in Coppeen, has a string of titles won over the last twenty years. Twelve Irish titles, sixteen Munster Senior titles, five Gold Celtic Nation titles, two EU Cup gold medals and in 2006 won the World Drug Free Power lifting title in Kinsale.

The most important organisation of all in the parish is the GAA. It was founded on the 1st November, 1884, in Hayes Hotel in Thurles by two men, Davitt and Cusack under the patronage of Archbishop Croke of Cashel. The GAA was only eleven days old when an energetic committee headed by the O'Riordans of Cooldaniel, the Murphys of Dromleigh and Dromeys of Dromcarra held the first GAA meeting in Toames near Macroom. Between those years and 1945 very little football was played in Kilmichael. But from then on Kilmichael began building a team. It was 1953 before they won the first Mid Cork title. This was the very first cup brought to Kilmichael, so it brought great honour and happiness to the people. In 1956 Kilmichael beat Canovee in Crookstown in a carnival tournament and were also presented with a cup. In the same year they qualified for the final of the Mid Cork Championship by beating Macroom in the semi-final at Coachford and later won the Mid Cork title by beating Donoughmore in the final. In 1957 Kilmichael were defeated by one point by Donoughmore in the replay of the Mid Cork semi-final at Coachford. Also in 1957 Muskerry created a surprise when they defeated a strong St. Nicholas team by four points, drawn principally from Canovee and Kilmichael. 1959 was another successful year for them in different sports. They won the Mid Cork Championship, but lost in the County semi-final to the Dohenys. On that year Mr. Ted Murray, Kilnadur was selected on the Cork team to compete in the Munster Cross Country Championships at Kilmallock, Co. Limerick. Also in that year the Kilmichael goal keeper, Donal Lehane, won the point twenty two rifle shooting contest at Macroom. 1960 was once again one of their glorious years when they won the Mid Cork Championship, but were beaten by Mitchelstown in the County Championships.

Kilmichael had very experienced players those years, one of whom was Sgt. Paddy O'Driscoll who was stationed at Tarelton and at that time was the Treasurer of the Cork County Board. In his earlier days he played with the Cork Garda Club as well as the Cork Senior Team, and was on the Cork team in 1956 and 1957 which lost both All-Irelands. On these same teams was a Kilmichael man by the name of Dan Murray from Toames. Other players who played for Cork were Jerry and Connie Murray, brothers of Dan, also Jack Lynch from Tarelton who played minor, and Denny O'Mahony also wore red jersey. In recent years Shane Prendeville from Toames played minor football for Cork. At present a player from the Nemo Rangers football club is proving to be one of the finest free takers and point scorers on the Cork Senior Football team, this is none other than James Masters, whose father Michael comes from Carrigboy. James is a very dedicated and highly talented player and was lucky enough to be picked on the All Stars team that travelled to Dubai in 2007. In hurling two players from the parish played minor hurling for Cork, Bishop Michael Murphy and Kevin Murray, Toames. In more recent years Kevin Murray, Kilnadur achieved All-Ireland success on the Cork Senior Hurling teams. Kevin's sister Aoife, who plays camoige with Cloughduv, played with the Cork Senior Camoige team that captured All Ireland Titles also.

In 1963 another Mid Cork title was achieved. Until 1982 Kilmichael had many lean years, but time was not wasted during those years, the club spent their time in providing a pitch, for up to then there was no special place for matches. Eventually they secured land in Anahala and with a lot of voluntary work, not only have they one pitch but they have recently completed a second pitch. An achievement to be proud of, for the upcoming generations. During the seventies the under-age teams were started which are of great benefit to the club. 1982 was one of the club's most successful years. The under-12s won their own division, the under-16s reached the semi-final of the County and were beaten by Kilshannig, the under-21s reached the semi-final of Mid Cork and the junior team won the Grade B Championship. In 1987 the Mid Cork Junior 'A' Championship came to Kilmichael. Under the captaincy of John Carroll, Gneeves, they beat Ballingeary in a thrilling game, but were beaten in the County Championship by Rockchapel in Milstreet. Up to the present day the club has won many titles, the most recent being in 2006, when they won the Junior 'B' Championship Final. The underage also have won numerous competitions, and this is due to the parents and mentors who put in so much time and dedication to bring the club to the level it is. In recent years Kilmichael have set up underage hurling teams in the Parish. Many of the older players played with Cloughduv over the years and achieved great success, so now hopefully they will build and develop a hurling team, that will take them to the junior ranks in the coming years.

Local Ghost Stories

The Two Rebels

Two rebels were being hunted by men on horseback. They managed to catch one man and tied him to a horse tail by the legs and dragged him along the road. When dead, he was put against a rock at a turn on the road and left there for a few days as his relatives were afraid to take the corpse away. His head is supposed to have left an indentation on the rock. The second man was hiding in the corn field, and all the horses spread out and walked through the field to look for him. One horse passed right beside where he was lying. The rider could not have missed him. It was either a miracle or the rider did not want to be responsible for another death.

Palace Anne Ghost – before 1858

The priest of Enniskeane parish lived above Murragh (where Dominic O'Sullivan lives now). A sick call came during the night. The priest went answered the call on horseback. When he was travelling from Murragh Cross to Palace Anne, a black dog consistently crossed in front of the horse. The horse could not kick him and was reduced to a slow pace. When the horse and rider crossed the river the dog disappeared. When the priest reached Enniskeane the sick man was dead. Thus they thought the black dog was the devil at work, as ghosts cannot cross water.

Ghost Story – About 1900

It was a bright summers evening and the sun was still shining in a blue sky. It was about 6pm and John who was working for a local farmer was driving the cows for milking. Another man was doing likewise, bringing in the cows, on a hill some distance away. They could see each other but were too far away to talk to each other. John heard a singing/crying noise over his head in the sky above him, and the sound was moving towards the other man. There was nothing to be seen. Just then, a Mrs. Doherty was dying. John and the other man were at her wake later that night and the other man had heard exactly the same as John.

The West Cork Railway

Introduction

The year 2006 marked the 45th anniversary of the closure of the Cork, Bandon and South Coast section of C.I.E. and the 30th anniversary of the last trains on the Cork City Railway. (It is also the 120th anniversary of the first trains on the Schull and Skibbereen narrow-gauge line.) The line ran from Albert Quay in Cork City to Bantry in the West, Baltimore in the South and Kinsale in the East, with many stops along the way. The construction of the railways took place mainly in West Cork between 1851 and 1893. By 1961, all West Cork railway lines were closed. Most lines closed in 1961, with the exception of the Kinsale Junction to Kinsale (closed Sept. 1931) and Ballinscarthy to Courtmacsherry (closed Jan. 1947). However the Ballinscarthy to Courtmacsherry Line was open to occasional seaside passenger excursions and Beet specials until the official closure in 1961.

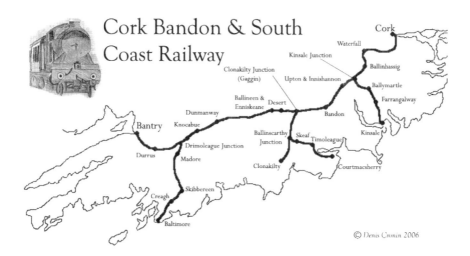

Cork Bandon & South Coast Railway

© Denis Cronin 2006

The West Cork Railway officially closed on March 31st, 1961. This date marked the end of an era which lasted over a hundred years. However, the closure of the railways left behind some momentous pieces of work; these would include the Viaduct which crosses the Cork-Bandon road, the Ballydehob Viaduct, and the many dilapidated train stations left across the county. Although there is less evidence to be found of the railway in West Cork, there are still many of the structures remaining, such as the train station in Ballineen.

The Journey

Below is an excerpt from *The Cork, Bandon and West Cork Railway – Vol. 1*, describing the journey westbound from Bandon in 1899:

> 'Our traveller settles down for the next stage of the journey, as the train climbs the embankment and crosses over Shannon St. then around the back of the town and past the now abandoned West Cork Company's station just beyond the long bridge under St. Patrick's churchyard. Soon, the train is passing Castlebernard platform, closed for some years to passengers, but still open to goods, as evidenced by the rake of wagons in the siding, serving Lord Bandon's estate. The main road runs parallel again for the next 3 miles to Clonakilty Junction. Here a good number alight for the branch train, waiting patiently in the bay platform. Our train now negotiates the crossover to the main line while the Clonakilty line goes straight on parallel to us under the bridge and veers sharply southwards. We cross a high embankment westbound, over what was once a trestle viaduct, continuing close to the Bandon River, and soon reaching Desert. Only one or two get off at this tiny station, and we see the mill siding going off at right angles on the up side. There are nice views along the river valley (which is now on the south side, having crossed it by a metal bridge just beyond Desert) as we speed along to Ballineen and Enniskeane, a new station opened in 1891 to serve the twin villages and sited mid-way between them. Originally there were separate stations, a little over a mile apart. Our traveller is now more relaxed as the train is less crowded, and he can cross to the opposite window as the train leaves to see the sidings and engine shed serving the ballast pit on the down side.

Now the train passes through a pleasant glade of trees for a few miles before passing Manch platform, closed to regular traffic since 1890, but still open for Baile Buidhe race traffic. Turning north-west, past Ballyboy level crossing and over the Bandon River by another girder bridge, the train soon reaches Dunmanway, quite a large station with up and down platforms and a busy goods yard. There is a lot of activity here as many more passengers alight, and a large number of parcels are unloaded. Soon the whistle blows and we are off again over the level crossing past the Railway Hotel, and Atkins Mill with its private siding on the up line.'

The Cork, Bandon and South Coast Railway
Vol. 1 – An Illustrated History by Colm Creedon

There were a number of different railway lines in West Cork. The table below shows the different lines, the stops on those lines, and the date in which they were constructed.

Lines	Built	Stops
Cork to Bandon	1851	Albert Quay, Waterfall, Ballinhassig, Crossbarry (Kinsale Junction), Upton, Innishannon, Bandon
Kinsale Junction to Kinsale	1863	Crossbarry, Ballymartle, Farrangalway, Kinsale
Bandon to Dunmanway	1866	Bandon, Clonakilty Junction, Desert, Enniskeane, Ballineen, Dunmanway
Dunmanway to Skibbereen	1877	Dunmanway, Knockbue, Drimoleague, Madore, Skibbereen
Drimoleague to Bantry	1881	Aughaville, Durrus Road, Bantry
Clonakilty Junction to Clonakilty	1886	Ballinscarthy, Clonakilty
Skibbereen to Schull	1886	Skibbereen, Newcourt, Hollyhill, Kilcoe, Ballydehob, Woodlands, Schull

Ballinscarthy to Timoleague	1890	Ballinscarthy, Skeaf, Timoleague
Timoleague to Courtmacsherry	1891	Timoleague,Courtmacsherry
Skibbereen to Baltimore	1893	Skibbereen, Creagh, Baltimore

The Closure

Good Friday, March 31st, 1961, is a date which will be remembered by many in West Cork. It was on that day that the government of the day, despite the greatest civil protest since the foundation of the State, closed the West Cork railways and the area lost a lifeline to the outside world. The closure was a sad day that marked the end of an historic era that had lasted over one hundred years. The West Cork Railway was never a big financial success; the reason for its closure being that it had accumulated losses of £56,000. It nevertheless provided a link for the people of the area with the rest of civilization at a time when there were very few cars, buses or lorries. The local railway station was the place where tearful fathers and mothers said goodbye to their sons and daughters as they left for the emigrant ship, and it was also the scene of many a joyous homecoming. The train had brought the good news and the bad news at a time when there were very few radios and no television, and it also brought the mail and the newspapers. All the commercial life of West Cork passed through the railway stations.

It was on June 30th, 1849 that West Cork's first train ran from Ballinhassig to Bandon, a distance of 10 miles. This was four months before the main Dublin to Cork railway opened. On December 8th, 1851 the section from Ballinhassig to Cork was opened. 300 men were engaged in the construction of the massive tunnel at Goggin's Hill, Ballinhassig, which was 900 yards long. The biggest task was the construction of the huge Chetwynd Viaduct, which can be seen today on the Cork/Bandon road. One thousand tons of steel was raised by special machinery to a dizzy height, and when completed, the huge bridge was 90 feet high and 440 feet long. It was indeed a great undertaking at that time.

The railway reached Dunmanway on May 1st, 1866, and the first train reached Skibbereen on July 22nd, 1877. Thousands had gathered at Skibbereen station from as far away as Mizen Head to catch their first glimpse of this mighty wonder. In 1881 the line was extended to Bantry from Drimoleague, and in 1886 it reached Clonakilty from Ballinascarthy. The final task was the extension from Skibbereen to Baltimore, which was opened on May 2nd, 1893. With the building of Baltimore Pier, the line was extended right on to the pier, and it brought a great measure of prosperity to the area.

Baltimore assumed a new importance. At the turn of the century there were three direct trains from Cork each day to Balitmore. The Mail Train which left at 5.15 a.m. and arrived at 6.15 a.m., the 9.20 a.m. which arrived at 12.30 p.m., and the 3.00 p.m. which arrived at 5.55 p.m. On Sundays there were two trains each way, and very soon these attracted day excursionists at cheap fares. Baltimore's annual Regatta on August Bank Holiday Monday attracted the greatest crowds of all. Even in the late 1950s as many as 1,800 people travelled by special trains to the regatta. The shock decision to close all rail services to West Cork was reportedly carried by a single vote at a meeting of the board of CIE on September 26th, 1960.

As soon as the news became known, the 'Save Our Railways Association' was formed, spearheaded in Clonakilty by Mr. James P. O'Regan, the well-known businessman and, in Skibbereen by Mr. Michael O'Driscoll, UDC. During the winter of 1960/61, practically every organization in West Cork met to protest and several public meetings were held. Dozens of resolutions were passed and sent to Dr. Tod Andrews, CIE chairman, and to the Minister, Mr. Childers, making both fully aware of the strong feelings of the people of the area. Despite mounting anger, the response from both CIE and the Government was negative and unbending. Their decision on the closure was final and irrevocable and they refused to discuss any scaling down of deferment of the decision. Some 37,000 signatures against the closing were collected at church gates. High Court action was commenced against the closure but had to be dropped when the plaintiff, Mr. James P. O'Regan, was informed that he would be held personally liable for all costs if his action failed.

So, on March 31st, 1961, the West Cork Railway was steam-rolled into oblivion.

Courtesy of *The Southern Star*, March 31st, 2001

Preparing for the Stations

This description of preparing for the stations just had to be written down, for how else would I remember the lovely sentiments expressed by this lady:

'Well they all came in the back door and I have my little houseen for the sticks and a little houseen for the wellingtons and boots and bit of storing and gatherums. Ther' only little stone houseens but sur you'd have to have them clean anyway, it saves the men bringing the muck inside if they throw their boots in the houseens. Then there's the jumpers; things that I throw up on the line there that I don't bother to put into the cupboards like gansies and cardigans and the aul raincoats; the houseens holds all them aul things.

Well I have corners cleared out that won't have to be touched again and I'll have a straight run through the middle of the floor the morning of the station; you know; you don't want people pulling at chairs out of the corners the morning of the station unless you had them cleared out.

A few bunches of flowers on the table will look grand and as long as they have a good plate of meat on the table; it isn't much else they'll want. As long as the place is clean and tidy; a good plateful and no foll dolls, nothing fiddly or fancy; a sliceen or two of tomato; my bit of pandy and no more about it. Once their bellies are full – ther' fine; Sur tis nice that all the neighbours meet each other; a nice bit of conversation, what more do they want?

You remember the old Canon? He always had to have his fruit; an orange maybe and he'd speak up looking for it if it wasn't in front of him; his own special fruit knife and a silver spoon'.

For the uninitiated the word 'Pandy' is simply – mashed potatoes:

'Pandy' always goes down well at the stations. The quality and taste of the 'Pandy' would vary in each household but for the most part, it was usually good. The smell of the chopped onions in the mashed potatoes was always more than one could resist: Floury potatoes were boiled and mashed with chunks of butter melting through the potatoes; milk or cream would be added, salt and pepper and chopped onions and the smell of the onions in the whipped creamy potatoes was irresistible.

The description of the salad above is still the standard fare that is served at stations.

I remember Canon Murphy reasonably well: I had never been to a station before until I came to West Cork; we were all gathered round as the Mass started, everything was going fine; Mass was over and my mother-in-law and her daughter went below to the room or parlour as it was called to serve the meal. Lo and behold – there was something missing. I heard the commotion and went down to look. The Canon hadn't yet gone down; there was my son going from bowl to bowl eating the red cherries from the top of the grapefruits. I made a swift retreat as the women ran out to the back kitchen to replace the cherries and picking up the chewed cherries as they went along. The day was saved and the Canon was none the wiser.

> 'The stations were always held at half past nine in the morning; the breakfast would always be a boiled egg and into the middle of the day you'd never think you had any station, they didn't make as much of it as they do today.
>
> We wouldn't have any breakfast that time until the station was over; there was fasting that time; the people would be on at half past nine and it would be over by half past ten; there was no tea and meat; there would be soda bread and brown bread and the priests would be delighted with it. The station used to run Tuesday, Wednesday and Thursday; not like now, they are scattered. When it came to Ash Wednesday, they'd start after that and they'd be all out of each other then, straight through each day – Kinneigh would be about the second week.
>
> The vestments and the station box used be shifted out and the Ballyvalone area was before us; the box would have to be ready when the priest would come in the morning. In olden days Canon O'Connell would come with a saddled horse; you

should secure the horse and feed it or you'd get a good rub if you didn't do it right. The Canon was the real old type of man; he was here in the late thirties. He was Parish Priest for about 18 years. He'd come to our school in Connaugh; he'd go in by Murray's and on down through Nyhan's fields and they'd have a gap open for him and when he'd arrive at the school they'd take out a chair for him so he could step up and down to the horse, he was very elderly you know.

All the Priests were very strict that time but he wasn't too bad after; for being in the parish so long, do you see, he was well in with all the neighbours around. The Curate; Father McSweeney was with him but 'twas the old Canon that collected up all the dues and Father McSweeney did all the work. Everyone knew of course what you had put up on the table. He'd call all the names and they went to the table with their dues they used no envelopes that time so they'd all see what you gave'.

I recall our own parish in another part of the country, where there were no stations but the dues were gathered up and the Parish Priest would call out the areas and the name of each person in the area and what they had contributed. The lowest contribution was a shilling and my Mother would give two and sixpence; this was in the late fifties and it was a day's wages which she could hardly afford. She wouldn't let it be said!

Canon Murphy was nice too; he was strict; he might say something straight out and it might not be what one would like to hear or expect to hear.

'Twas hard that time starting Mass at half past nine because the milking had to be done; the cows out and the dirt off the yard; you had to have it cleaned before the Priest arrived; there was no running water then to clean it or cement yards; you had to be up at six and fasting from midnight and there'd be no breakfast until after the Mass.

You only fast an hour now and people make too much of a thing about the stations. There might be a bottle of stout back then, and drink would not be given out nearly always until after the Priests were gone. The Priest wouldn't stay long that time – they wouldn't want any drink on them for they might fall off the horse. Of course you'd have a bottle of something in the house,' twas cheap you know and people couldn't afford much. The stations were always a great thing for you'd do something to the house.

All the preparations that time were very plain, we used old fashioned paint and a bit of whitewash, they wouldn't be worried about toilets for no one had them. Many the chairs that were sat on; still had damp paint and there should be plenty of stories of when this happened – it was hard to get up from a newly painted damp chair!

The butterballs were memorable to many for the making of these was an art in itself. It was hard work; the butter balls were made with little wooden spades and I still have them in the house, I took them from home with me when I got married; everything would have to be very clean: the spades were put into hot water and then cold and the piece of butter put in between the two little spades and you'd work the spades around the butter to make the balls and it could still go again you, they were nice but ridiculous. It was a lot of fancy but you know it was done out of respect for the Priest it was all 'the Priest' – times have changed an awful lot that way; sure the Priests are very friendly now – you were on edge that time, trying to be up and doing and not make any mistake. It isn't so much that they were demanding but that you'd like to have things the best way you could, people were kind of afraid of them I suppose you'd say.

People would be excited about having the stations: There was a man one time having the station and he was watching out for the Priests so that he'd be out to greet them; he saw them coming and hurried out the door. The yard had been washed the night before, so it had been wet when a heavy frost came; in his hurry to meet the Priests, he ended up sliding along the yard and ended up in front of them on his backside; when he got up he turned around to the Priest and said; if we get any more skeates like that sure we wont be long skeating into Christmas!.

We'll take our yard that time; there were no cement yards and you'd have the dung outside the stall so there was a bit of clearing up in it, there was terrible excitement'.

I have seen for myself and have it on good authority that there were major efforts in order that all the outhouses and the house and walls would all be gleaming of whitewash and dressers, tables and chairs were painted and a new oil cloth put on the kitchen table. There was a white table cloth put on the table that was the altar for the Mass; a white cloth for the table down in the room; the station box was collected from the house that had it last. The white cloths still stand but we no longer need to collect the box; the priests have cars now and the money is put in envelopes.

'The last job was in the morning; ferns and grasses were spread out around the yard to clean it up; that was in the thirties, forties and fifties, the cement yards did not come in until the sixties.

You had the Mass and straight after, the dues were collected and you had to go around and ask everyone if they'd like to stay for a cup of tea.'

'You'd be talking about the Priest; the old people that time were as odd as the Priest; you'd have to make sure to tell everyone to stay for breakfast; some could be gone the road out and then they'd get insulted, and the thing then- if you met them the following day- how were they going to be met; they'd be saying how they didn't even get a cup of tea in the morning. It was always the case that the men were always served first for the breakfast with the Priest and the women would get a cup of tea while they were waiting. The tables were cleared away when the men were finished and the ladies sat down; as you know that's all changed now.

There wasn't as much drink then, maybe an old woman might have a little glass of sherry on the quiet. The cooking was done on the open fire; the kettle was boiled hanging on the crook over a good fire and the eggs were cooked in the saucepan on the side; the women sat around the fire and they'd ask us to hold the toast as we sat around the fire. They were very particular about looking after the Priest. The Priest would come on a horse and later on, a cart and then the car. Some neighbours brought their cart if there was an old person to be carried. My Mother Lord have mercy on her often came to the convent gate to collect us from school in the pony and car; that was the nicest spin we ever got, sure that was all the go that time; two could sit in front or sit in the back and we'd be delighted.

Father O'Connell had a great interest in farming: he knew all about farming, he had a piece of land himself. If things were going right they'd be thankful. It was a fright to keep the place clean on the day: the Priests wouldn't take any notice as much as we would for we had no tarmac or cement yards only a rough stony lane'.

The Fair of Ballabuidhe

'Twas early in the morning as the sun rose in the east,
I set out for Dunmanway by my side a handsome beast.
I soon joined up with others and enjoyed their company,
As we led our horses to the sale, at the Fair of Ballabuidhe.

As we approached that Doheny town the crowds all gathered there.
I found myself a vacant spot at the north side of the square.
And I stood there with my handsome mare as the bidders came to see,
But I held tough as the day was young at the Fair of Ballabuidhe.

Chorus:
It is a fair beyond compare there's no one can deny,
Selling, buying, drinking, fighting the limit is the sky.
Tanglers tinkers three-card-tricksters all join in the spree,
For a cob or a mare or a booze-up rare it's the Fair of Ballabuidhe.

The bids came fast for our white mare and we made a bargain fair,
With a spit on the hand and a slap on the palm the deal it was sealed there.
Our throats were dry and our spirits high so the Kearney's I did lead,
And we raised our glasses in a toast to the Fair of Ballabuidhe.

The night came down as we roamed the town and visited each bar,
The drink was neat and the tunes were sweet so we sang and danced our share.
But all good things must end they say and so it came to be,
But we vowed right there that we'd meet next year at the Fair of
Ballabuidhe.

Repeat Chorus

© Colum Cronin (CCR Music 1984)

The Fair of Ballabuidhe is held annually in Dunmanway town on the August Bank Holiday weekend. Primarily a Horse Fair, this event has also been an important social occasion for generations of West Corkonians. I wrote this song based on personal experiences and conversations I recall which occurred between my father and his compatriots.

The accompanying illustration was drawn by my brother-in-law, the late Paddy O'Neill (Glounthaune and Bauravilla).

Seanfhocail

Is fearr an tsláinte ná na taínta
Health is better than wealth

Moll an óige agus tiocfaidh sí
Praise the youth and she will come (and they will flourish/bloom)

Aithníonn cíaróg ciaróg eile
One beetle recognises another beetle / It takes one to know one

Níl aon tinteán mar do thinteán féin
There is no hearth like your own / There's no place like home

Is binn béal ina thost
The quietest mouth is the sweetest / Silence is golden

An rud is annamh is iontach
That which is rare is wonderful

Is maith an t-anlann an t-ocra
Hunger is a tasty sauce

Is minic a bhris béal duine a shorn
Many a time a man's mouth broke his nose

Tús maith leath na hoibre
A good start is half the work

Is leor nod don eolach
A hint is sufficient for the wise

Ar scáth a chéile a mhairimid
We all exist in each others' shadow / you cannot live on your own

Is maith an capall a tharraingíos a charr féin
It's a good horse that pulls his own cart

Is fearr Gaeilge bhriste, ná Béarla cliste
Broken Irish is better than clever English

An áit a mbíonn mná bíonn caint,
agus an áit a mbíonn géanna bíonn callán
Where there are women there is talk,
and where there are geese there is cackling

Coppeen Grotto 1954–2004

50th Anniversary Commerations – 8th December 2004

Our Lady's grotto in Coppeen was built in 1954. It is located on the road-side just west of the village on a site which was donated by the O'Driscoll family. Colonel PJ Coughlan of Manch was the architect who designed the grotto. Neily Warren was the building contractor, while Mick Cosgrave was the main tradesman, tended by Jack Hurley, with Jack Dwyer and others. White quartz stone was gathered from surrounding farms. This supply was soon exhausted, but fortuitously a large quartz stone was blasted on Michael O'Driscolls land in Liscroneen, and the resulting stones were collected and drawn by Barrett's lorry, finishing the construction of the grotto.

Fr. Ml. Nolan P.P. leading prayers at Coppeen Grotto on 8th Dec. 2004, commemorating its 50th anniversary.

© Colum Cronin 2004

The statue was made by an Italian, whose shop called 'Bernardos' was located in Paul St., Cork. Ned Barrett transported the statue from Cork, resting it carefully on top of a load of ration bags. When he arrived in Coppeen, there were many helping hands to get it off the lorry. The cost of the statue was £30.

The 8th December 1954 was cold, with an easterly wind blowing bits of snow. It was market day in Ballineen. A cortège assembled in the school-yard, and proceeded in a procession to the grotto, where a large crowd awaited. Fr Pat Cahalane performed the dedication ceremony.

Two lilies from Madge O'Callaghan's were planted in front of the grotto. In more recent years, two miniature trees were planted at the back by Michael Buckley Mountmusic.

On the 8th December 2004, a group led by Fr. Ml. Nolan P.P. gathered at the grotto to commemorate the 50th anniversary of the building of the grotto.

The Grotto Building Committee included:
Feenie O'Driscoll
Breda Barrett
Eileen and Sheila Hurley
Jackie and Tommy Collins
Florence Con O'Driscoll
Mary Crowley (Malachy)

Piséoga

There is a little rhyme if you see one or more magpies:

One for sorrow, Two for joy,
Three for a kiss, Four to die,
Five for silver, Six for gold,
Seven for a secret that's never been told

Another variation is 'Three for a girl, four for a boy'.

If you saw a single magpie, to negate the sorrow, you would give the magpie a wave.

If the palm of your hand is itchy, it is a sign that you will get money.

If the side of your nose it itchy, it means someone is talking about you.

If an item of cutlery falls, it means you will have a visitor calling.

A robin flying into the house is an omen of ill fortune, in some places is a sign of a death in the family.

If you open up an umbrella in a house, it is bad luck.

When you enter a house, you should leave by the same door that you came in.

It is unlucky to walk underneath a ladder.

If you threw a dead animal into your neighbour's field, all your bad luck would be passed on to them.

It is lucky to stand on the grass in the dew on the May morning.

If you stand on the ditch between farms on May Day (1st May), you take all the milk from your neighbour for the year.

If you meet a foxy woman on the way to the market to sell, you should turn back straight away, because you won't sell anything!

If a dark (haired) person is the first person to enter a house on May morning, it is lucky for the family.

If you can hang your hat on the moon (when the lower point of the crescent is facing upwards), it is a bad sign of the weather for the month.

If the whitethorn is out before the blackthorn, it is a sign of a good summer.

Jack the Lantern: This was an old piséog which was blamed if you managed to get lost in a familiar place: My grandmother told me a story where she got lost in a country area familiar to her while she was cycling as a young lass. Somehow, she missed the turning she was supposed to take, and suddenly realised she was disoriented. After a while she came upon an old man at the side of the road. She opened her mouth to ask for directions, and at that point, she realized she knew exactly where she was, and so said to the man, 'I took the wrong road.' It is thought that if Jack the Lantern causes you to lose your way, the spell is ended the second you talk to anybody.

The Harvest

The grain crops primarily grown in Ireland were wheat, oats and barley. It was cut anytime from the 1st of August to the 1st September with a reaper and binder. The binder bound small bundles of corn, approx. 2.5 – 3ft long with twine. These bundles were called sheaves. The sheaves were then made into stooks. A stook was made up usually of six sheaves. A person held two sheaves, one under each arm. The head of the sheaf which contained the grain was faced back and the base of the sheaf faced forward. They were placed on the ground about a foot apart, base down and the heads pressed together. Then two more sheaves were placed against these, until there were about six to eight sheaves in a bundle together. They balanced on one another which allowed air to circulate through thus allowing the corn to dry and ripen.

The stooks were later made into stacks depending on weather. This was a specialist job as the rain had to be kept out for a few weeks. The stack was about 8 feet in diameter and about 10 feet high, coming into a peak like a spire on top. The stooks were taken apart and a single sheaf placed on the ground. The 8-foot circle began at this point and each sheaf was placed on top of the other until a cone shaped design formed which reached 10 feet in height.

The corn was then drawn into the haggard, which is a yard, and made into a reek. A reek was about 14 feet wide at the base, 20–40 feet long and about 20 feet high tapering into a few feet at the top. The size of the reek depended on the amount of corn you had. Two reeks were built with enough space between them to allow a thresher to fit. They were covered with rushes until the engine and thresher arrived.

A threshing set consisted of a steam engine, a thresher, and a small caravan on wheels to carry equipment. Threshing day was a big event. The steam engine and thresher pulled in the night before. The owners of the thresher and their workmen usually slept at the farm house that night so as to rise early, as it took a few hours to raise steam in the engine. Then the whistle was blown and neighbours began to arrive. Different jobs were

Pictures courtesy of Pat Murphy

John Crowley's steam threshing set working in Cronin's Munigave in 1939

allocated to different men; about fifteen would have to be on hand to start. There were four men piking from the reek to the thresher. Five men on the thresher, one feeding the thresher (the owner of the thresher or his workman), one on each side of him cutting sheaves and handing them to the feeder and two men piking to the cutters. This process allowed the grain to be separated from the straw. The grain went down shoots into bags at one end of the thresher and the straw went out the other end to be made into a reek. There were three men on the ground taking the straw from the thresher and making a straw reek. This reek was considerably bigger than the previous two reeks before the thresher, as it contained the straw from both these reeks. Again, it was a specialist job. The reek was then covered with rushes. Then sugáns (ropes made with straw) were made, and thrown over the reek with a weight at each end to keep the reek firm and straight, as it had to keep out the rain for an entire year.

Threshing day was also a big day for the women. Meat was bought from the butcher the day before and lovely green cabbage also. A pot consisting of 10–12 gallons of potatoes was boiled over the open fire. Neighbouring women came in to help. Straining the potatoes was a big job, usually left to the man of the house. The pot was hanging on the crane, and a big bag was put on top, and the pot turned sideways allowing the water to spill out. A keg of porter was 'tapped' and distributed in an enamel jug to all and sundry. There might be a bottle of whiskey for the 'special people'. People had to be counted and there were usually a few sittings for meals, which called on the organisational skills of the women in charge.

Captain Francis O'Neill

M id way, in the western side of Kinneigh old graveyard stands an impressive Celtic Cross headstone monument. Many people have remarked on the mention of Brian Boru etched on the inscription here. Taking a closer look at this inscription beckons the reader towards a fascinating story which lies behind this grave, its occupants and in particular, the individual who erected this memorial to his grandparents. Firstly, let us take a close look at the inscription. It reads as follows:

ERECTED BY
Colonel Daniel Francis O'Neill
Chicago USA

TO THE MEMORY OF HIS GRANDPARENTS
Daniel O'Mahony (CIANACH)
DIED APRIL 1857, AGED 80 YEARS
and **Mary O'Mahony (CIANACH)**
DIED JULY 1857 AGED 78 YEARS
A GIANT IN STATURE AND A LEADER BY NATURE
O'MAHONY MOR – **"THE CIANACH MOR"**
WAS A WORTHY DESCENDANT AND REPRESENTATIVE
OF **MAHON SON** OF **CIAN** AND **SABIA**
DAUGHTER OF **BRIAN BORU**
REQUIESCANT IN PACE AMEN

(Daniel) Francis O'Neill was born on August 28, 1848, the youngest of seven children in the west Cork town land of Tralibane (near Bantry). The son of a well-to-do and educated farmer, 'Frank' and his siblings were spared from the ravages of the Great Famine that devastated the western regions of Ireland.

O'Neill grew up in a largely Irish-speaking rural society in which music, song, and dance were an integral part of life. His parents, sisters, and himself, were all great singers; and his parish supported two professional pipers in the years after the Famine. At a young age, Francis began learning the wooden flute, a skill that would stand him in good stead some years later.

At the age of sixteen, he was given a letter of introduction to the local bishop. His family sent him off to a life as a priest but he had a change of mind and ran away to sea. He circumnavigated the globe and was later shipwrecked in the Pacific. He was rescued and landed in San Francisco. He did some ranching in Montana before going to Chicago by way of New Orleans and Missouri. In Missouri, he married a young lady, Anna Rogers, whom he had met when she was an outbound passenger on one of his voyages from Ireland. He and his wife moved to Chicago in 1870, shortly before the Great Chicago Fire in 1871. He came to Chicago to work as a sailor on the ore boats that cruised the Great Lakes. Fate intervened and the Captain ended up as a patrolman on the Chicago Police force. He was on the force less than a month when he was shot by a burglar. He carried the bullet, lodged near his spine, until his death. Even though he was

© Colum Cronin

wounded in the shoot-out he still managed to arrest the felon and bring him into the station. Not a small feat when you consider that patrolmen in those days walked their beat.

The Captain gathered many of Chicago's Irish musicians in an organisation called the Irish Music Club. With the help of the Club and James O'Neill, his nephew, he began to collect and publish Irish Music. He also became a champion for the music as revisionists started to make claims that the music might be of origins other than Irish. His response to the suggestion that the English dancing master, Playford, was responsible for writing some Irish tunes was impressive. With the help of many devoted collaborators, O'Neill collected well over 2,000 tunes in manuscript, which would result in several published works. The most famous of which was the 1903 publication of O' Neill's Music of Ireland. Containing 1,850 melodies, it was the largest collection Irish music ever printed. The Captain's papers and reference materials are archived at the University of Notre Dame.

Chief Francis O'Neill died on January 26, 1936, but the musical tradition that he revived lives on forever in his hometown Chicago, in his native Ireland, and in Irish communities all over the world.

Captain O'Neill was the General Superintendent of Police in Chicago at the turn of the 20th century. He preferred the title Captain, to Chief or Superintendent, which perhaps give us some insight into the man. By any measure he led an exciting life.

He returned for a holiday to his native land in 1906. It was during this period that he organised the erection of this gravestone in Kinneigh. The exact location of residence of his grandparents remains a mystery to this writer: (it has been suggested that they lived in the Kinneigh / Coppeen area) His mother (their daughter) lived in Castledonovan before she married O'Neill.

Gurranreigh Famine Monument

Between 1845 and 1850, more than a million Irish people starved to death as a consequence of the failure of the potato crop, while massive quantities of food were being exported from their country. Half a million were evicted from their homes during the potato blight, and a million and a half fled to America, Britain and Australia, on board emigrant 'coffin' ships, many of which were old, overcrowded and disease ridden.

Before the famine, this area in the south-eastern corner of Kilmichael Parish had a large population including a thriving village (called Cathairach which was home to up to five hundred people). During the famine, this village and a huge percentage of the population of the area were practically wiped out by hunger, disease and emigration.

A *Cork Examiner* reporter gave this harrowing report on his visit to Gurranreigh in 1847:

> 'As you pass along the road you see none of the indications of industry that formerly might be seen on every side – you see no fields dug up or ploughed up – no labourers working by the roadside – no cottages springing up – all seem uncultivated and desolate. Nothing meets the eye but untilled fields and tenantless hovels, almost crumbling into ruins, and haggard skeletons, the very shadows of what had once been strong and cheerful peasants.'

Four members of the Hanna family of this townland were found dead in their cabin (close to the monument) in an advanced state of decomposition. The mud cabin; which was thatched, was tumbled in around them so that the earth and debris was mingled with the bodies before an attempt could be made to bury them. Rev. James O'Driscoll P.P. Kilmichael came to administer the Last Rites to these victims. Looking around him, he realised that many of those assembled were also weak with hunger and disease. He therefore consecrated some ground in the town land to save people having to travel to Kilmichael Cemetery some 5 miles away to bury their dead. The only signs of this once thriving village are the foundation stones of the mud cabins on the O'Mahony farm in this town land.

A monument was erected by Kilmichael Historical Society near the location of the village as a reminder of Ireland's most tragic human disaster, and its stark consequences on this area.

Author & Historian Michael Galvin giving a talk at Gurranareigh Famine Monument on Sunday 4th Sept. 2005

Kinneigh in 1904

The boy to man initiation rite around Kinneigh in 1904 and for years to follow was not specifically sexual, pugilistic or febrile but to clamber up the ivy of Kinneigh Tower and circumambulate its narrow stoned rim. The first reference to this site was in the *Annals of the Four Masters* for 850, i.e. 'Fortbasach abbot of Cill Mor Cinnech died'. Dated to the eleventh century the old people believed that this magnificent structure could only have been built by the Goban Saor himself. Decapitated at the top, its face is uniquely hexagonal with a door 11 feet from the rock foundation and six chambers in all, rising to over 70 feet, Kinneigh was once a bishopric founded by St. Mocholmoge or Columba and the present church was build in 1856. The famous footprint nearby is said to be that of the saint when he jumped in anger from the top of the tower when a cow was stolen from the monastery by robbers. The place name Kinneigh is an anglicized corruption of Cíonn Eich or Ceann Each (head land of the horse). The cloigtheach or bell tower survived into the 19th century. The tower's bold stance on an elevated rock outcrop and with its high door was designed to ward off foreign and native marauders eager for the spoils of a more civilized settled community, i.e. gold and silver ornaments, sacred vessels, coin, wine, leather and other goods of valued currency, that in the early medieval milieu only the church had the learning and motivation to generate and produce.

John Crowley manager of Castletown-Kinneigh Creamery circumambulated the tower or so he told Benjamin Herriot on a cold December night in 1904 in Eddie Forbes' public house. Benjamin Herriot was visiting his cousin the local rector Canon John Hayes. He too could claim a thing or two of distinction but not on this particular night, as he had just recovered from the lashing pangs of what the French call *coup de soleil* or *delirium tremens* from many years of chronic alcohol abuse. In Forbes' also that night was John Sullivan, Garlands, whose son Danick was day and night asking his father about Christmas, as that of 1903 was the first the child could consciously remember to do with festive treats. No such joyous seasonal anticipation existed in his father's time. It was only now at the beginning of the new century that an increased emphasis on paedocentric or child-focused thinking was noticeable. Children were now slowly beginning to be appreciated more for themselves than as objects to be made fit into a high Victorian adult milieu. Though the Christmas-tide Santa Claus was still a way off yet, children could now expect some modest treat, an apple or sweets in a hanging stocking. Previously children were not only neglected and abused but worked relentlessly partly out of ignorance, partly out of a necessity in the immiserated society of the disadvantaged classes.

By the fire that night too was Maurice Donovan, Coolabana, holding up his calloused palms to the fire, hands knarled from years of hard work; building ditches, draining bogs and intermittent road contracting. He knew what a day's work was and the hunger that follows such toil but he also knew how to take brief time out to relax, imbibe and converse. 'Hanam an Diol,' he meaningfully exclaimed, 'the praties 'ud want to be well earthed up tonight with that grey frosht, 'tish for rain I'd say but thanks be to the Almighty God a Thiarna 'twash not like lasht year a terrible year altogether. Yes, too the praties 'ud want to be covered well tonight with the besht rushes in the portach'. The others present nodded in monosyllabic agreement, with Eddie Forbes remarking, 'Twash the blue shpray men, the blue shpray that shaved the praties and the people.' Another patron of Forbes', Joe Cummins, Ardkillen, described great hardship up the West Coast where 'they are not ushed to ushing the blue shpray'. All this he had heard from the local school teacher Miss Burke, who read it aloud from the *Cork Examiner* in O'Mahony's post office, Castletown-Kinneigh.

Extracts from the book *Pure Pride* by local author Michael Galvin

Pad O'Mahony

The rural landscape of West Cork has undergone considerable change over the past 200 years. The Ordnance Survey map of the 1840s for the townland of Munigave shows a patchwork of tiny fields averaging about one to two acres in size, spread about each farm unit. The small fields were an product of the previous 100 years as Irish agriculture moved from pasture based to one where tillage dominated. The open spaces associated with common grazing were replaced by enclosed fields to aid drainage, limit windborne weed infestation and protect crops from grazing livestock.

Another feature of the 1840s map is the many small dwellings, located seemingly at random around the various farms. If you look at the 1840s Ordnance Survey Map each farm was punctuated by several such small dwellings, single storey houses, usually built of mud.

About 30 such houses existed in the townland of Munigave East, in addition to about 6 farmhouses, supporting a total townland population, according to the 1841 census, of 253 people. Each farm had a number of these houses. These were mainly the dwellings of labourers who worked on the local farms. In a cashless society, the rent for these cottages was paid with a number of days labour on the farm and a half acre or so to grow enough potatoes and keep an animal to feed the family for most of the year. Hunger was never far away and such cottagers bore the brunt of the catastrophe that ensued when the potato crop failed in 1845.

One character who inhabited one of these cottages at Munigave during most the 1800s and into the early 1900s was a man named Pad Mahony. The site of his cottage can be seen in the photograph above – the small plot surrounded by trees in the lower part of the picture, where the laneway swings right away from the forestry plantation.

Pad survived the many upheavals of the 1800s. He was not entirely typical of the inhabitants of these cabins. He was a tinsmith by trade, a skill learnt from his father. He never married, so there were not many mouths to feed, a factor that may have helped him survive the famine.

Pad's cottage had the usual 'half acre' attached to it. I remember my father growing potatoes on it in the 1950s, long after all remains of Pad's cottage had gone. Undoubtedly, potatoes had been grown in the same plot for a century or more before. But, being a tinsmith, Pad could trade his skills for money and so was fortunate in not being completely reliant on his potato crop.

When Pad died in 1911, no one knew how old he was. He used to tell a story of once going to Macroom as a child with his father and seeing the severed heads of some executed rebels on display from the walls of the castle, a practice that did not last much past the early 1800s.

More extravagant stories suggested Pad even remembered news of the Battle of Waterloo reaching West Cork. Stories such as these were used to estimate his date of birth as sometime during the Napoleonic wars. The civil registration index for Dunmanway district records the death of Patrick Mahony in the autumn of 1911, aged 106 (PRO reference 5/159).

The census of 1901 tells a different story. Pad may have left it to the census enumerator to estimate his age and he is recorded as only being 70. There are many of people being less than candid with the census enumer-

ator, particularly about their age. Perhaps the answers were influenced by the fact that the enumerator function was usually carried out by the local RIC officer. However, Pad progressing from 70 in 1901 to 106 in 1911 is one of the more spectacular examples.

The stark census details profile Pad – occupation tinsmith, fluent in English and Irish, unable to read or write. Depending on which statistic is correct, Pad Mahony was born sometime between 1805 and 1830 and his 1901 census record would have been typical of many Irishmen of the time, possibly the last generation to be genuinely bilingual. His inability to read or write speaks of a childhood spent before the National School System reached Coppeen.

Pad's occupation of tinsmith would have seen him doing a lot of travelling around the district. Much of his trade would have been carried out either visiting individual houses or attending local fairs and markets. It is easy to see the travelling tinsmith as a bearer of local gossip and stories of earlier times. If he entertained his clients he might be rewarded with a better meal. It was probably our grandmother who heard and believed his stories and passed them on to her children. She would have known him from her teenaged years until he died.

Griffiths Evaluation shows Andrew Mahony as one of the tenants on what later became the farm where I was born. Two other Mahony families occupied cottages on the farm. One of them was probably Pad's father, although, according to Griffiths' map, none of them lived in Pad's cottage. As a bachelor son, Pad would not have been mentioned in Griffith's Evaluation. Pad's stories of Waterloo and the severed heads in Macroom Castle might possibly have been his father's memories rather than his.

By the time Griffith's Evaluation for County Cork was published in 1852 to begin the property taxation system known as the 'Rates', the famine years had already devastated the neighbourhood. There were now only 23 inhabited households in Munigave East. Another 7 unoccupied dwellings are reported.

Some houses had disappeared altogether and, according to the 1851 census, the population of Munigave had declined by over 50% in the decade since 1841. The population of the whole country had declined by almost 2 million in the same decade.

By the turn of the 20th century, Pad's cottage was the only such small dwelling left on our farm. The local Rural District Councils, Dunmanway in this case, were beginning to provide a more modern alternative in the form of stone built cottages on half acre plots acquired from farmers. My great grandfather was paid all of £10 for the land on which one such cottage was built in 1899.

When Pad died in 1911, the various Land Acts of the 1890s and 1900s had finally eliminated the landlord and tenant system that had dominated and blighted the rural economy of Ireland for so long. My grandfather, along with all the other farmers in the area, acquired 'In Fee' ownership of his farm in 1908, and Lord Bandon's agent no longer collected the rent.

Pad Mahony had lived through all these changes. From my aunt's recollections, Pad was being partly supported by the Wood family in his old age. He was fed from the family kitchen. While still a small child, it was my aunt's duty to walk down the laneway to his house with his cooked dinner each Sunday, a distance of a few hundred yards. His house was on the edge of the bog, now the Moun Rua forestry plantation, and Pad was forever warning her of the dangers of playing in the bog.

One relic of Pad's life has survived. After his death, his tinsmith's anvil was housed in one of the outhouses of the Wood farmyard. In the 1950s, when the farm was sold, my father gave the anvil to a neighbour, who still has it.

My aunt, all of six years old at the time of his death, was taken to see Pad's body after he died. She remembered seeing him laid out in his coffin in the kitchen of his cottage, dressed in a brown shroud. She listened to the debate that was held about what age to record on his death certificate. Sometime in the 1980s, she related these events of her childhood to her son. By the time my aunt died in 1999, not far short of two centuries of Irish history had encompassed these two overlapping lives – from pre-famine Ireland to the rise of the Celtic Tiger.

The Fair Day

There was a tradition of selling cattle in the springtime, taking them out of houses (not the fields) and going to the fair. Ballineen was considered to be one of the best fairs in the area, maybe due to the railway being close by. On the day of the fair, we would start at 4 or 5 o'clock in the morning. This meant a day off from school so we would be delighted. Usually it was yearling cattle we prepared for fair day, they got extra mangolds and barley and were in good condition and well presented for their journey.

I remember the neighbours meeting at the cross, coming along from the north with their groups of cattle. Sometimes it was pre-arranged to group with another farmer, but mostly it was spontaneous. Then off we went, up the hill and down along towards Castletown. Sometimes the women might come along to help at the early stages of the journey before we met another group of cattle, then they would return home, safe in the knowledge that we were capable of managing.

There was always a horse and cart with the troupe; it was available so that if someone got tired, they could hop on for a rest. Different groups would join us along the way so that we might end up with 10–15 people and maybe 30 cattle in a group.

It was pitch black dark at this time of the morning, and several Storm Lanterns were used to show the way. The cattle were fairly docile in those days, and were relatively easy to handle. Nevertheless, you had to be alert, as there was always a risk of having an animal wander off in a wrong direction, maybe in a lane or gap, then the others might follow. The cattle were usually fairly tired by the time we got to the fair.

As we approached Ballineen, near the end of the School Line, the 'jobbers' would be there waiting for us. Their ambition was to persuade the cattle owners to sell their animals to them as cheaply as possible before they entered the fair proper. If they succeeded, they would simply take the animals down the road and sell them on at a profit, repeating this process as often as possible. The Landlords would also be about; they travel by

train and stay in Frank Hurley's Hotel in Ballineen the night before.

The cattle that were purchased by them would be driven towards the train station. All the doors of the houses and shops would be closed in case the cattle would enter. (It was told that an animal once went into a house and up the stairs but failed to turn on the landing) Special wagons were available at the railway station for cattle, each wagon was filled, holding about 20 cattle. All the buyers would have their own scissor mark to identify their cattle (like branding).

One day for some reason, my dad didn't sell one cow, a white heifer, but when he went looking for the heifer to take home, it had gone missing. He checked the railway wagons and sourced his animal, created a fuss and managed to get it unloaded, which took some determination! He always brought an animal home, even if he sold all of his own, he would purchase a couple more, maybe a smaller one or a slightly sickly one, and then fatten them up for the next fair.

My dad held his own special spot at the fair, more from tradition than anything else; this was at the gable end of Farrell's Shop. I still remember holding the cattle there for the day until they were sold. By evening time when the cattle had been taken away by the buyers, we were given a few pence each and were let free to go shopping. We were taken west to a place called 'The Eating House', which was owned by a Mr. Buttimer, which was just west of Tisdall's corner. That was one of the highlights of the day for us. Then we headed for Pompy Shorten's Shop, where we used to buy old second hand American Comics like Roy Rodgers, and Beanos and picture comics. My brother Donal hoarded them under his bed, and he wouldn't part with them for all the tea in China! Another popular post in Ballineen for the fair was William Foley's Yard. People used to hold their cattle here until they were taken away by rail. The yard was divided up into pens. There were very few trucks in those days, most of the cattle were transported by rail, or walked home if they were bought by locals.

I remember the following day, when we went to school, we would explain our absence to the teacher, explaining that we attended the fair, and there would be no trouble. In fact it appeared as if Master Crowley admired fellows who took a day off now and then to partake in learning from the 'University of Life'.

Local Placenames

Cappeen   Caipchin – Little wood clearance, crest of a hill. At the east is Knickaunavoughalla – Cnocan Ui Bhuachalla (O'Buachalla's hillock) near which there are cromlechs called O'Boughalla's Bed and O'Boughalla's Grave. At the west side is the large ring fort of Cahirvagliair – Cathair Mhagh Gliadhaire (fort of the plain of the warrior) which was one of the chief residences of the Cineal Laoghaire.

Moneygaff   Muine Gamh – Thicket of the winter streams, place exposed to bleak winds. It might read Muine Dhamh – Thicket of the oxen or male deer. At south side is Moinroe Bog – Moin Ruadh (red bog)

Lackanashinagh Leacain na Sionnach – Hillside of the foxes.

Moneynacroha   Muine na Croiche – Brake or thicket of the gibbet. The actual site of the gibbet or scaffold is at a spot called Barra na Piece – Top of the peak.

Ballyvelone   Baile Bhile Eoghain – Place of Owen's sacred tree.

Barnadivane   Bearna Ui Dhubhain – Devane's gap or defile. It might read Bearna Damhan – Gap of oxen, cattle rearing place

Slieveowen   Sliabh Eoghain – Owen's hill. At the north side is Labbaowen – Leaba Eoghain (Owen's bed or resting place).

Lackareagh   Leaca Riabhach – Grey or furrowed hillside.

Teerelton   Tir Eltin – Eltin's land. The townland may have a connection with St. Eltin who lived mid 6th century.

Garranereagh   Garran Riabhach – Grey grove

Kinneigh   It derives its name from Airchinneach Mor, a Cineal
                  Laoghaire chieftain. In this townland was Kinneigh
                  monastery. the old cemetery remains as well a the bases
                  of the monastery walls. At the south side is Castle rock
                  and in the townland are a number of gallans. Part of the
                  monastery grounds was termed the Abhalghort or
                  orchard.

Slieveowen Wedge Tomb

Slieveowen wedge tomb, also known as Labbaowen, is located in the townland of Slieveowen just to the north west of Coppeen village. Take the road at the side of the former Post Office, beside An Caipin Bar, along the Fuscia walking route, details of which are available in the pub. Through the cross roads you will see some forestry on your right with an entrance way. Follow the track to find Labbaowen. Leaba is a common prefix for these monuments which were once thought of as giants' graves, with good reason considering their size.

As with all old stories there is usually a germ of truth somewhere. In this case the idea of the structure being a grave. The original burial or burials were of cremated remains placed in pits inside the wedge shaped stone tomb. More than one person could be buried here.

They are called wedge tombs because of their shape, in profile and in plan; see fig. 1 below, a drawing of an excavated wedge tomb in Island, Co. Cork. From the side the wedge tomb is higher at the end where the opening is and tapers towards the rear. It is the most numerous type of megalithic tomb in Ireland. Nearly all megalithic tombs in Co. Cork are wedge tombs. In terms of age, these tombs were built between 5000 and 3500 years

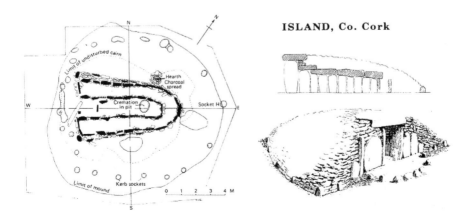

ISLAND, Co. Cork

Inchincurka Wedge Tomb

ago. In some cases they continued to be used as burial sites into the medieval period.

Labbaowen represents the earliest known man made construction on our local landscape. Nothing older has yet been recorded. The unhewn stones that form the tomb were moved into place to create a long gallery or chamber, 3.7m long and 1.35m wide at the west end and 0.3m at the east end. Large cap stones were then placed on top so that, generally, they sloped upwards towards the gallery opening and entrance. Labbaowen is oriented ESE-WNW. The usual orientation is south westerly. Today Labbaowen is in poor condition, the surrounding forestry robbing it of its view. The trees were planted very close to the tomb and this has resulted in damage to the surrounding area. Sometimes these monuments were covered with a cairn of stones, see fig. 1, it is not clear if this was the case at Labbaowen. It stands between 700 and 800 feet above sea level.

Thinking about a structure that is one of the oldest on our landscape makes me ask myself many questions, for example:

Who built Labbaowen?
Why were these people here?
How did they live?
Where did they come from?

Labbaowen, Slieveowen
© Colum Cronin 2007

Wedge tombs are associated with 2 of the most significant developments in mans history: (i) the beginning of farming and (ii) the creation and use of bronze.

About 5000 years ago people in Ireland began to change their lifestyle from hunting and gathering to a way of life more focused on agriculture, rearing animals and cultivating crops. Land had to be cleared to allow farming. These people invested time and energy in the land, work that needed a well organised community. Wedge tombs were probably focal points for these groups or tribes. The building of which would have created a sense of community and focus, a shared goal. It brings to mind the grottos built in the Marian year. Many of these grottos consisted of quartz gathered throughout the parish and brought by the members of that community to a place that was going to have special meaning for them. A place to be together. The burial of an important tribesman or relative in such a monumental way possibly was a means of marking territory and also creating bonds within the community. These tombs and their construction reflect a change in how society was organised.

Labbaowen is the first recognisable burial we have in our landscape
Labbaowen is the first recognisable burial we have in our landscape. This
goes together with the idea of a community settling down to farm, being
tied to one place, no longer nomadic. Burial, marked by the creation of a
wedge tomb like Labbaowen, was a new departure. Multiple burials have
been found in some of these tombs. But only enough to suggest that specific or special people only were buried here. Not everyone was buried in
a wedge tomb. Sometimes only a little cremated bone was found, maybe
an offering or symbolic gesture to a god?

The distribution of megalithic tombs in Europe is very interesting. They
are very numerous in France, Southern Spain and Portugal, western
England, Wales and Scotland. What connects all these places? The sea.
Open water is much more conducive to movement than a forested landscape hiding the unknown. The deep cut peninsulas of west Cork and
Kerry must have been very inviting to anyone arriving by boat from the
Atlantic coast of Iberia and France. Undoubtedly movement took place up
and down these coasts, and with goods and people go ideas and inter trib-
al relationships. And so it is thought that the tombs may have come up the
Atlantic coast, not physically of course but as an idea, a concept, a design
and plan. Brittany in France is seen as the most likely place of origin for
Irish wedge tombs.

Along with farming the creation and use of copper and bronze is associated with the society that built wedge tombs. Certainly they both appear
around the same time. Indeed a hoard of 6 copper axes of an early type was
found in Coppeen itself. And not too far away in Clashbredane near another wedge tomb, Bredanes Grave, another hoard of 25 copper axes was
found. This points to a community in this vicinity either producing or trad-
ing these items. It is thought that surface copper mineral deposits were
exploited to produce the metal needed to create these early axes. In the
beginning a copper axe was probably an exotic prestige item, a status symbol, rather than a working tool. But eventually they replaced polished
stone axes completely and were used as tools. A copper axe had a number
of advantages over a stone one. If it broke it could be fixed or recycled and
it was more efficient.

Gold objects were also produced in the south west of Ireland at this time.
The items made in this early period, about 4500 years ago, were gold 'sun
discs', small round decorated sheets of gold. Sometimes they had perfora-
tions at the centre suggesting they were stitched onto something.

This is the context within which Labbaowen was built. It was a product of a community who had taken up farming and settled down in our area. They made their own tools using the resources around them. They were the first people, according to current knowledge, to have made a visible mark on our local landscape, maybe as many as 5,000 years ago. Labbaowen is still visible today. The next time you take the Fuscia walk-way, take time to have a look at this monument. Visit what just might be the grave of one of the very first inhabitants of this area, Owen, who gave his name to both the townland and the giant's grave.

Wakes and Funerals

In the old days when people died after midnight, the wake would be held in the house the following day and night, and the next day, when the corpse would be taken to the church about 3pm in the hearse. There were no funeral homes, no ESB and no motor cars in those days. At that time all the neighbours would come together and help out. When a person was sick, some would come by day and a many more by night.

When a man died, a delegated man from the area would come and shave him. Then you also had two women from the locality to lay him out. All three of those would be in attendance for the occasion. The corpse would be laid on a bed with the legs in the washing bath. The women needed the assistance of a male if the corpse was heavy. The body was washed carefully and then dressed in undergarments. At that time a shroud would be worn over the other clothes. If death was imminent, a shroud would be purchased beforehand. They could be bought in those times in any local shop. Some shops would have them blessed, but if they didn't, you would have to take it to the priest to bless it. Brown was the colour of the shroud, and it looked like a long dress, and was from neck to the toes. It was the same for both men and women. Some of the older people would have it purchased years in advance. In the summer months, if you went in to a yard, you could see a shroud out on a hedge, or a limb of a tree, being aired and kept fresh, in readiness for the fateful day.

As the two women were preparing the corpse, a man would be sent to a designated house in the locality, for the 'waking sheets' Those sheets were not used for any other purpose. One was put on the bed and the other on the back frame of the bed behind the head. In those times, there were a lot of piseógs; the same man who collected those sheets had to take them back to the house once they were laundered. I remember one summer, when a man was collecting the sheets at about six in the morning, he was passing through a yard, and the dog alerted the lady of the house. She guessed he was collecting the sheets, so she got up and as he was coming back with the sheets, she stopped him from coming in to the yard. It was said at that time, if you carried them through a yard, it would be the next house for those sheets.

There was a very large attendance at night time wakes. The rosary would be said at midnight, by a designated person from the area, usually a woman. In my area, it was a man, and it would take fifteen minutes longer, as he would be calling on every saint to pray for the corpse, I would sometimes wonder if all of them were authentic! When the rosary was over, some people would go home, but more would stay until morning. The corpse would always be accompanied throughout the night. If it was a young person, it would be very sad and lonely, but if it was an older person, there would be more craic.

On a bedside table next to the corpse lay a lighted candle, snuff, cut tobacco and clay pipes. Strips of paper were provided to light the pipes. The story is told of a son (slightly inebriated) of an elderly man who passed away, lit the clay pipe, put it in the corpse's mouth and said, 'Here, old fellow, take a pull of this. If you are in Hell, we can do nothing about it now.' Then there was the family who had gone to mass on their donkey and cart, while there, the old man had died, while sitting on a chair. His head was stooped down, so it made it harder for those laying him out. The room where he was laid out was narrow, with the bed in the centre. So to keep the man's head in place, a pair of brown laces, the same colour as the shroud, was produced. They were put around his neck and tied back under the sheet to the frame of the bed. One of the women, who laid him out, had told her son about this. Her son went up to the corpse and sneakily cut the laces with his penknife. This caused the head to pop up, and all of the people made for the door in fright.

In those days, when the hearse arrived, the coffin would be placed on two chairs in the kitchen. The undertaker would always bring an assistant with him. On one occasion the assistant was just eighteen years of age, and it was only his second funeral. The house they were in, had a turn in the stairs, and the corpse was very long, so he had to be lifted over the banister. If the person was not sick for too long, wind might escape with all the movement. As it did escape, the young fellow almost collapsed with fright, as he thought the man was not dead.

When preparing the grave, the gravediggers would first have to cut the sod. This would be done with a spade or a hay knife. It would be the length and width of the grave, and in one piece. Next a timber stake would be placed on the sod, and then the sod would be rolled around the stake and taken by two men in a horse and cart to the grave yard. When the grave was filled, the sod was rolled back on top and this covered the grave. The first funeral I saw was in 1941. The hearse was followed by a side car, drawn by a horse, next was a regular horse cart and then seven saddle horses, and no motor vehicles.

That's my experience of both the living and the dead.

Cars Over the Last Fifty Years

The Baby Ford was the first Ford car that had a solid front axel. The Ford 100E Prefect was the first of the independent front suspension and that model was unique in that it had a vacuum wiper assembly. Then came the Ford 105E Anglia, which was a very popular car. Then the Cortina, followed by the 1600E, which was a lovely well-finished car. After that, came the Capri, the Sierra and Corsa which were bigger model cars. The Fiat model competing with the Ford's were Fiat 1500, 1100, 850 and 600. Then came the 124 and 128.

The first of the earlier Austins, A35 and A40 had a dual system brake with cable working the rear and fluid working the front. The mini Austin was the first of the front wheel drives in the smaller car with engine and gearbox together.

I drove Austin's and Morris's because they suited the pocket, even though I worked in the Fiat Star Garage in Bandon. All my friends were driving Fiat's on which I did nixers. There was always someone there to give a hand as Belrose had become a great scriochting centre.

Then the Volkswagon (VW Beetle) was the only car which had an air cooled engine so no water was necessary to cool it. This allowed the engine to be removed very easily.

Today's cars are all gone electronic. Electronic ignition, windows, airbags, keys, alarm systems etc. They were easier to fix in the old days when there was less to go wrong!

Tractor and lorries seen at Carlow Sugar Factory in 1928
Picture courtesy of Ned Barrett

Kilmichael Ambush

During the War of Independence, which started around January 1919 and ended in July 1921, numerous officers in the Royal Irish Constabulary, which was Ireland's British established police force, were resigning at an alarming rate. Then Sir Hamar Greenwood, British Chief Secretary for Ireland decided to reinforce them with a ruthless force of battle-hardened British Auxiliaries. Each man carried with him a rifle, two revolvers and a Mills bomb. In August 1920 about 150 of these Auxiliaries took over Macroom Castle and made it their barracks.

Around 2:00am on Sunday morning November 28th 1920, a group of Volunteers were assembled north of Enniskeane at Ahilnane. Fr. O'Connell P.P. Enniskeane arrived on horseback and heard their confessions. Then they marched cross-country towards Kilmichael, passing close to Coppeen village. They paused briefly at a house in Lissicurrane where buckets of tea were provided. Pat Deasy a sixteen-year-old from Kilmacsimon and John Lordan, Newcestown joined them later. They were deployed thus:

The Command Post occupied by Tom Barry with Jim (Spud) Murphy and John (Flyer) Nyhan, both from Clonakilty and Mick O'Herlihy from Union Hall.

No. 1 section: consisted of 10 men, north of the road.
No. 2 section: Michael McCarthy from Dunmanway led 10 more, who were situated behind the monument.
No. 3 section: Stephen O'Neill was in charge of 12 men, who were divided into two groups of six, at either side of the road. Two unarmed scouts were posted at the northern side of the ambush and another on the Dunmanway side.

Around 4.05pm on this wet and cold evening, the tired and hungry volunteers got the signal. Two Crossley Tenders carrying eighteen Auxiliaries commanded by Colonel Crake were approaching the ambuscade. Tom Barry wearing a military officer's tunic stood on the road facing the first lorry. As it slowed down, he blew his whistle and threw a Mills bomb in the cab of the open lorry, killing the driver. No.1 section fired and soon all occupants were dead. No.2 section attacked the second lorry, the Auxiliaries jumped on to the road, and as is widely believed, shouted 'surrender'. Most historians agree that in response, three inexperienced volunteers stood up to take the surrender and were treacherously shot. The three volunteers, Michael Mc McCarthy, Jim O'Sullivan, Rossmore and Pat Deasy, who died later and were regarded as martyrs ever since, were temporarily buried in Gortroe, but were later interred in Castletown Kinneigh. In reaction to this, Barry ordered his men, to open fire again on the Auxiliaries, and in the ensuing exchange, all but two of the Auxiliaries were killed. Of the survivors Lieutenant Cecil Guthrie was captured near Dromcarra and executed. He was buried in Anahala bog, and years later reinterred in Inchigeela cemetery. The other Lieutenant (Cadet) H.F. Forde was rescued the following day at the Ambush site, and taken to Macroom for medical aid, and subsequently to England. It is believed that Lieutenant Forde lived into the 1980s though paralysed and confined to a wheelchair.

Ambush Monument

© Colum Cronin 2006

Barry marshalled his men, sent for a doctor and priest. Fr. Gould, C.C. Kilmichael, attended the wounded and dying. They collected rifles, revolvers and ammunition, and then burned the two lorries. Before marching his men southwards, he lined them in front of the rock, ordered them to present arms and salute their fallen comrades. Arriving in Granure, about 11pm, they sheltered in a vacant cottage, where they were given buckets of hot tea and buttered brown bread, and were able to rest their weary bodies. They eventually dispersed and returned to their homes in West Cork. Midday on Monday, three lorries arrived from Macroom to collect the dead. In reprisal they destroyed and burned houses and hay barns around the locality and fired shots at various people. Kilmichael Ambush has been heralded as one of the best-planned engagements ever in guerrilla warfare. In 1966, the now famous monument was erected, with script in both English and Irish and in part, reads as follows: 'They shall be spoken of among their people; the generations shall remember them and call them blessed'.

FOOTNOTE: Sir Hamar Greenwood was chief Secretary for Ireland between 1920 and 1922; he followed in the footsteps of James Ian Macpherson.

The grave at Castletown · Kinneigh   © Colum Cronin 2005

The Auxiliaries

The Auxiliaries were recruited as a para-police force, following the departure of the RIC from most country barracks. They were officers who had fought in the First World War, and publicised as the very best of England's fighting men, and were established as a terrorist force to wipe out all the resistance to British rule in Ireland. Highly paid and often undisciplined, they were heavily armed, each man carried a rifle, two revolvers and a Mills bomb. The names of the Auxiliaries involved in Kilmichael on that day were:

William Barnes; Cecil Bayley
Leonard Bradshaw; Francis Craik
James Cleave; Philip Graham
Cecil Guthrie (escaped from Kilmichael, but captured nearby at Dromcarra and shot); W.Hooper-Jones
Fredrick Hugo; Albert Jones
Ernest Lucas; William Pallester
Horrace Pearson; Arthur Poole
Frank Taylor; Christopher Wainwright
Benjamin Webster and H. F. Forde (The only survivor)

The Volunteers

At Kilmichael Tom Barry's men included:
Jack Aherne, Budrimeen, Ballineen. Sonny Carey, Dunmanway. Neilus Cotter, Kilnadur. Batty Coughlan, Dunmanway. Denis Cronin, Gurteenroe, Bantry. Sonny Dave Crowley, The Paddock, Enniskeane. Timothy Crowley, Glounbrack, Reenascreena. Pat Deasy, Kilmacsimon, Bandon (died at Kilmichael). Sean Falvey, Ballymurphy, Innishannon. Johnny Hegarty, Keelinga, Leap. Jack Hennessey, Cahir, Ballineen. Michael Hurley, Brade, Union Hall. Dan Hourihan, Girlough, Ballineen. Jack Hourihan, Toureen, Skibbereen. John Lordan, Coolnaugh, Newcestown. Jack McCarthy, Lissane, Drimoleague. Michael McCarthy, East Green, Dunmanway (died at Kilmichael). Paddy McCarthy, ('Kilmallock') Kilcoe, Ballydehob. Timothy 'Casey' McCarthy, Durrus. Jim 'Spud' Murphy, Pearse St., Clonakilty. John 'Flyer' Nyhan, Clonakilty. Denis O'Brien, Castlelack, Bandon. Paddy O'Brien, Girlough, Ballineen. Tim O'Connell, Ahakeera, Dunmanway. John O'Donovan, Behigullane, Dunmanway. Michael O'Donovan, Bonagh, Rosscarbery. Michael O'Donovan, Cullane, Leap. Patrick O'Donovan, Drominidy, Drimoleague. Patrick O'Donovan,

Author Meda Ryan delivering the oration at the ambush site in 2005

Inchafune Hse, Dunmanway. Dan O'Driscoll, Kilvurra, Rossmore. Michael O'Driscoll, Snave, Bantry. Michael Con O'Driscoll, Granure, Ballygurteen. Jerome O'Hea, Lissycremin, Lislevane, Bandon. James O'Mahony, Ballineen. Jeremiah O'Mahony, The Paddock, Enniskeane. Denis O'Sullivan, Ardfield, Clonakilty. Jack O'Sullivan, Cahirmounteen, Kealkil. Jim O'Sullivan, Knockawaddra, Rossmore (died at Kilmichael). John D. O'Sullivan, Bawngorm, Bantry. Jack Roche, Kilbrittain. Ned Young, Dunmanway. John Kelly, Johnstown, Kilmichael (Southern Scout). Tim O'Sullivan, Shanacashel, Coppeen (Northern Scout).

Kilmichael

A parish that is partly in the Western Division of the barony of East Carbery, but chiefly in the Barony of West Muskerry, was originally called Uibh Flann Luadh or Iffanloe (the territory of Flann). Situated between the towns of Macroom and Dunmanway, it is the second largest parish in the Diocese of Cork, stretching 17 miles in distance. In political terms, it is now in the North West Cork Constituency.

General Tom Barry

The youngest of eleven children Tom Barry was born on July 1st 1897. He attended National School at Ardagh Rosscarbery. He worked as a clerk in Bandon until 1915, then joined the British army and during World War 1 served in the Middle East. On returning he enrolled in a business college in Skerrys. In 1919 he joined the West Cork Brigade of the IRA and was appointed as the Brigade Training Officer and from that, organised the Brigade's Flying Column throughout the War of Independence. He was briefly imprisoned in the Curragh Internment camp. In 1927 he worked for the Cork Harbour Commissioners. He was Chief of Staff of the IRA between 1936 and 1937, but retired from the IRA in 1938. During World War 2 he was Operations Officer in the Irish Army in the Southern Command. His book *Guerrilla Days in Ireland* was published in 1949. General Tom Barry died in the Mercy Hospital Cork on July 2nd 1980, and was survived by his wife Leslie Bean de Barra.

Crossley tenders

These vehicles were built in Manchester, they were mainly 3 ton, and 4 x 4 vehicles with 4 cylinder engines. Francis and William set up Crossley Brothers in 1867, when Francis, with help from his uncle, bought the engineering business of John M Dunlop, William joined him shortly after the purchase. The company name was initially changed to Crossley Brothers and Dunlop. The brothers were committed Christians and strictly teetotal refusing to supply their products to companies, such as breweries, that they did not approve of. They adopted the early Christian symbol of the Coptic Cross as the emblem to use on their road vehicles. The business flourished and in 1881 Crossley Brothers became a private limited company.

The Mills bomb

In 1915 William Mills a Birmingham engineer developed this grenade. It had a central spring-loaded firing pin and spring-loaded lever locked by a pin. When it was in the air, the lever flew up and released the striker, which ignited a four-second time fuse allowing the thrower to take cover before it exploded. When the grenade went off the cast-iron casing shattered producing a shower of metal fragments.

Short Stories

Escaped Patient

There was a fellow named Sean who would stay only a week or two in any one place. He would travel from place to place, working his way around. He kept his clothes on his back, in a non returnable ration bag. One time, he got a job in the mental hospital in Cork. In that job, you got a jacket to wear, with your name and a number on it. This man was put in charge of four patients in the yard of the hospital. When they were called to dinner, he took in the four lads, and he came back out himself, and struck for the road again. As he was coming out the Carrigrohane Road, a farmer was digging spuds. On the gate of the field was sign, 'Potato pickers wanted'. So Sean went in, met the farmer, and was told to go picking. After a few minutes, the farmer saw men making for the gate and pretty soon, they were all gone except Sean. He went over to Sean, who was bent over picking the spuds, to ask him if he knew what happened when he saw on the jacket; Sean, Number 10, Mental Hospital, Cork. All of them thought he was a patient after escaping.

A Ghostly Trick

Sally Leeson was murdered in Roughgrove in the 1800s. Her ghost haunted the old road but only came as far as the river. Ghost stories were being told the night of the threshing. Two ladies, Lena Whyte in her early twenties and Agnes Hurley who just made her confirmation decided to play a trick. They went to the river, Lena stayed behind in the bushes. Agnes put on a white dress and held a lighting candle in front of her and put her veil down over the candle. Three or four men were standing at the cross roads on a beautiful moonlit night. Agnes walked out from the river and the men started running, each in his own direction. Their hob nail boots could be heard running on the road for miles! Sally Leeson had crossed the river!

The Killing of the Pig

L ong ago most farmers would kill a pig annually. Some might even kill two or three, especially if they had a big family, or had someone working for them. Meat was scarce in those times, as people would not go to town as regular as they do now. They would normally cycle or go by horse and cart.

The first pig I saw being killed was in 1940. At that time every farmer had a large table in the kitchen for the day of the threshing. That would be taken out to the yard for the killing. The fat pig would weigh about eleven stone. There was a designated man in each area to kill the pig, and often he might be the only one in two or three town lands, that would be capable of such a job. He had a special knife for the job. It had a blade of about 10 inches and a 6-inch timber handle and was known as 'The Bleeder'. This knife was kept especially for this purpose.

He brought with him a rope, about 6 feet long, made a loop of it and put it in the pig's mouth, to hold him down. Four strong men would put the pig on the table, on his back, each holding a leg. The butcher would hold the pig's head with the rope. With a good edge on the blade, he would cut the skin on the throat, down the middle, and go about 3 inches deep. He would then stick in the bleeder and cut a vein and the pig would bleed to death. The woman of the house would have a bucket to collect the blood. She would have salt in the bucket, and would keep stirring the blood with her hand until it was cold, otherwise it would coagulate and be no good. Oaten meal and onions would be mixed with it, and then it would be baked in the bastible for one hour.

When the pig was dead, a 40-gallon barrel of hot water was near the table. The farmer would have got two churns of it from the creamery that morning. The pig would be dropped in the barrel to clean the hair off, pulled back out, and then the other half dropped in. This was difficult work, lifting the pig, as the legs would be very slippery when they were wet. The last of the hair would be cleaned off with knives. He was then hung up inside a house from the rafters by his back legs. Next his head was

Síle Murphy 2007

cut off and was then opened down though the centre of his belly, all the guts were taken out and thrown away. The heart and liver were boiled, all the head was eaten, right down to the bone, ears, tongue, all except the eyes. The crubbeens were a specialty, a pub in Cork city was well known in song and in story, for its crubbeens. It was known as 'Cathy Barrys'; the owner would get a bag of crubbeens, from the bacon factory and boil them. Sandwiches and crisps were not available to accompany a pint back then. Crubbeens were easily served, no wrapping of paper, no knife or fork, only held by your fingers and eaten to the bone. The bladder was taken from the guts, cleaned, washed and dried. Then, it was pumped like a football and given to the children to play with, much to their delight. At that time every bit of the pig was used except the intestines. It was then washed out with water drawn from a spring well. Two sticks were put in to his sides to keep him open for the night.

The next day, it would first be cut in two parts, taken back in to the table and cut in to manageable portions. About three stone of salt would be used to preserve the meat. The bottom of the barrel was filled with salt, the meat put in, topped up with salt again, and left in an out house. The meat would then be covered with bags and heavy stones, to keep it in its place, as the salt melted to form pickle. So when the pig was thoroughly pickled, it was toasted with a few drops of poteen, and a good meal was enjoyed with some pudding.

I killed a lot pigs myself. When I started, it was easier, the table and boiling water, were no longer used, the pig was killed on a high footpath, and the pig's head could drop about a foot, so his blood would flow in to the bucket. At that time I had two light ropes, each about 16 inches long. A rope was put on the back leg first and then on the front, and then the same on the other side. You then would have a handle about 18 inches long, you put the handle under the rope and wound the handle until the pig's four legs came together and had the pig resting on his back. One man could hold the pig then. So the job could be done with two men less. When the pig was hung up on the rafter, you had two horseshoes to tie his legs to. I then had a blow lamp, to burn the hair off the pig, which would take about half an hour, the result was a black pig, so a soft brush and some cloths were used to scrub it clean. The pigs at that time, had long tails, but nowadays they have hardly any tails, so the pigs now are going with the modern times. If at the present day you were caught stabbing a pig by a Department Official you get six months in prison for animal cruelty. However, one human can stab another and get off scot free. I still have my 'Bleeder' well worn, but still with the same edge, as it had, almost eighty years ago.

Kinneigh Tower

Tower rises
'neath evening sun
Swallows swerving, gliding
In clear blue sky
Twitters sing in every branch
Stately trees shimmer in the breeze
Doves coo contentedly in overlapping branches
Their sheltered nests sway softly midst the busy bees

Far away traffic hums to and fro
Nothing spoils the stillness of this green floor
Except the hungry crow
Raucous cackling calls from treetops
Guard over all the residents below.

Old headstones covered in moss smelling of bog
Humps that sink and rise while here and there
A stately stone leans over
Guarding there that piece of ground wherein
Holds the bones of precious souls
Priceless heritage underground
A simple cross of iron
A stone, a tomb, some clearly state who lies within
I feel sorrow deep for the unmarked grave

Side by side; just a wall between
Ivy clad entry for souls to walk through
Generations of Protestants peacefully rest
Close by; lye their Catholic brethren
In solemn ground lie
in the shadow of the tower

I leave by the iron gate:
My mind full;
Unanswered questions
Behind those ivy clad walls
Quiet ghosts
Remain

Surnames

Ireland was one of the first European countries in which a system of fixed hereditary surnames was developed. Most Irish surnames are derived from Gaelic and Norman names. English and Scottish names also occur to a lesser degree. A common feature of Irish surnames is the O or Mac prefix which originally meant 'son of' e.g. Séan Mac Murchadha would mean Séan, son of Murchadha. When the Irish language declined in the 18th and early 19th century, it led to a gradual drop in the use of these prefixes. However in the latter part of the century, these prefixes widely came back into use. Nowadays, many variations of the same name can be found, with certain forms are used more widely in the areas where they originated, while other variations of the same name are found elsewhere.

Murphy: The surname Murphy is one of the most common surnames in Ireland. The name derives from O Murchadha or Mac Murchadha in Irish. However, the 'O' prefix is not in use today. The greatest Murphy clans were from Co. Wexford and in particular Counties Cork and Kerry. The Munster sept is associated particularly with the barony of Muskerry, Co. Cork. The name is still numerous in Co. Tyrone, but even more common in Co. Armagh.

Crowley: The surname Crowley in Irish is 'O'Cruadhlaoich', derived from 'cruadh' meaning hard and 'laoch' meaning hero. A branch of this sept settled near Dunmanway in West Cork, and later became a distinct sept at Kinshallow. Many became soldiers, usually fighting for the MacCarthys. Almost all Crowleys are now found in Munster, with over seventy five per cent of these in Co. Cork.

Hurley: The surname Hurley is derived from the Irish 'O hUirthile', but in some cases has also been rendered Cammane, from camán, the Irish for a hurley (stick). The majority of present day Hurleys are from Co. Cork, as was the case in the seventeenth century, when the name was also recorded as numerous in Counties Limerick and Clare.

Kelly: Derived from the Irish name O'Ceallaigh, from 'ceallach' which could translate to either bright-eyed or troublesome. The surname is common throughout Ireland while also one of the most popular in the country after Murphy. The prefix 'O' was dropped during the period of the Penal Laws, but was largely revived at a later stage.

Walsh: Again, one of the most popular surnames in Ireland. Derived from a semi-translation of the Irish word 'breathnach' meaning Welsh. It has similar origins to the surname Wallace, originally derived from the Old English term 'waelisc' which was used to denote native Welsh or Britons.

Larkin: In its Irish form O'Lorcáin, most likely derived from 'lorc', meaning rough or fierce. It is numerous in the areas where it originated, including Galway, Monaghan, Tipperary and Wexford.

Lordan: In Irish form Ó Lórdáin, this surname is almost exclusively a Co. Cork name, and numerous in the western part of the County.

Cronin: Derived from the Irish name Ó Cronin from 'Crón' meaning brown or swarthy. Croneen is a more accurate rendition of the original pronunciation. Hereditary owners of the territory west of present day Clonakilty. Also the leading families were eranaghs of Googane Barra. Most commonly associated with Cork, especially West Cork.

Kelleher: Derived from the Irish Ó Céileachair, from Céileachar, meaning 'uxorious' or overly fond of one's wife. The original family claim descent from a nephew of Brian Boru. Originally from Co. Clare, the Kelleher's moved to southeast Cork in the 14th century, and are now most commonly found there and in the neighbouring county of Kerry.

Galvin: The surname Galvin, or O Gealbhain, is derived from the words 'geal', which means bright, and 'ban', which means white. They were originally found in County Clare where they held a family seat. Variations of the name include O'Galvin and Gallivan.

Barrett: Mostly associated with the Cork and Mayo/Galway areas, where two separate Barrett families settled. The larger of the septs settled in Cork, but were of less importance than the other sept in Gaelic times. The name is thought to be of Norman origin, meaning 'son of Baraud'. The Irish form of Barrett is 'Baróid' in Munster, and 'Bairéid' in Connacht.

Cohalan: This is believed to be a variation of the surname Coughlan, derived from 'cochal' meaning cloak or hood. It is believed that the Cohalan's originated in Co. Offaly.

Kingston: This surname is believed to be of English origin, although very numerous now in County Cork. Surveys in the 1800s saw around 90% of Kingston's residing in Co. Cork. Kingston is thought to be a mistranslation of the surname MacCloughry, from cloch (stone) and rí (king).

Donovan: Derived from the Irish 'donn' meaning brown, and 'dubhan', a variation of dubh meaning black. Originally found in Co. Limerick, the O'Donovan's descended from Crom, who built Crom Castle, Co. Fermanagh.

Carroll: Derived from the Irish 'cearbhaill' meaning 'warlike champion', or maybe 'brave in battle'. Of Irish origin, it has a number of different variations, including O'Carroll, Carrol and Carol.

O'Mahony: Derived from the Irish Ó Mathúna. When translated, it means descended from Mahon, or 'Bear-Calf'. Descended from Mathúna who was the son of Sadbh, Brian Ború's daughter. Numerous in West Cork.

Country Life in the 1930s

The type of farming carried out was mixed, mainly dairying, livestock and some tillage, such as barley, oats, wheat, mangolds and also potatoes, turnips, and cabbage. Cows were milked by hand, milk was separated on the farm in a special clean dairy, made into butter in a churning barrel. The butter was packed into firkins of four stone barrels, sealed and sold at the local market in Dunmanway to buyers from the butter exchange in Cork City, where it was exported to America and the British Forces in India. The skimmed milk was fed to pigs and calves. The cattle and pigs were sold at Ballineen and Dunmanway fairs. The cattle were walked to the fairs, pigs and bonhams were taken in a creel (like a horse and cart). They had an early start to the day they went to the fair. Cash exchanged hands during these transactions.

The horse was the tractor of the time, horse and plough tilled the land, the cereals they produced were brought to Canty's Mill in Enniskeane in 1930 and to Barrett's in Coppeen in later years.

It was stone ground, some was sold and the remainder brought back and stored for winter feed for the animals, the ground wheat was used for bread making. The Canty's mill was water driven by hand pumps.

The farmer's wives kept poultry for egg production, they also bred turkeys and geese reared and fattened for the Christmas market which was held locally, sometimes a travelling huckster would call to the farmyard to buy them, it was a very exciting time. Farmers grew their own vegetables and potatoes, so in the Spring, say March and April, the cutting of the 'scillains' for the potato planting was done in the farm houses by the local women. Pigs were killed and cured as required, the farmer's wife would make some homemade black puddings from the pig's blood and would add oatmeal, onion and spices, and it was absolutely delicious. In the early 1930s–1950s, the travelling creamery came along to collect the milk from the farmers; it would stop off at Gloun Cross. The horse and cart would be tackled up to take the churns of milk to one of these stops and it was also a great meeting place to catch up on the local gossip.

In the summer, the farmers and some local men went to the bog to cut the turf. It was cut into sods with spades, laid out on the banks to dry, and when dry it would be put into stacks and later drawn home in a horse and crib or butt, put into sheds for fire in the winter. The open fire was the only source of heating with turf and timber, although in later years, some coal was burned too. Coal was delivered to Ballineen train station and collected by the farmers. They also delivered coal and turf to the schools. All the children walked to school, often barefoot in the summer time, usually through the fields. No form of transport was available for them at that time.

Letter writing was the only form of communication; post was delivered three days a week, the postman walked to deliver the post until he acquired a bicycle. The price of a stamp for an ordinary letter was 2 pence.

This is a far cry from the communication technology of today, with telephones, mobile phones, faxes, computers and the internet. People were very happy with their lot in those days.

In June before silage was ever thought about, the hay was cut in the fields with a horse and mowing machine, then turned, raked and put into cocks by men, then drawn into the haggard with a horse and sleigh and into a shed, to be fed to the cows and cattle in the winter. Another job to be done in the month of August was the cutting of the corn. This job was also done with the horse and mowing machine, cut into sheaves, bound, and put into stookes. Usually the stookes were built into stacks which were meant to be weather-proof. Later, these were drawn into the haggard, and built into a large reeke. On the day of the threshing, the steam engine would arrive and a meitheal of men would gather from the neighbourhood to help with the work, such as putting the sheaves into the thresher. The oats and barley came out the other end. The men would bring the bags on their backs into the barns. The straw would be put into a reek and used for feeding and bedding the cattle in the winter. This was a very big occasion when the threshing was over. The men were fed and had a keg of porter to drink from. There would be a big sing song and dance until the early hours. All the farmers helped one another for the threshings.

The stations were another big event. They would be held in Spring and Autumn. The farmers would do a big clean up in the houses, inside and outside, the station would start with nine o'clock mass in the morning. The parish priest came on horse back to the station. After mass, they were given a large meal and plenty of drink. It would finish up with a singsong and dancing with all the neighbours participating.

The travelling cinema would call around during the winter months and stop off at Gloun and Coppeen Cross for a week at a time, a very welcome diversion, as there was no television then.

Dancing at the crossroads, or the pattern as it was called, was held in the summer months, on Sunday evenings. There was many a good night of dancing in Shanacashel School or sometimes an old empty barn where local musicians performed. All the courting was done on the way home under the bushes. There were no motor cars; the girls were taken home on the crossbar of a bicycle.

The women at that time never visited the local pub, but on some occasions where they partook of a little shebeen and snuff it could be a match making event as it was there most of the matches were made.

House weddings were the norm at the time, the couple would get married in the local church in the brides parish at about nine or ten o'clock, come back to the brides home, where the party would go on until the early hours of the morning, for some couples there would be no honeymoon, just back to the groom's home for more celebrations.

The lighting in the houses was in the form of an oil lamp, with paraffin oil the fuel used in them. Candles were another source of light, standing them in a 'sconce'. The next was the tilly lamp, a great light, until electricity came in the fifties, which started off with the Lee Scheme at Inniscarra where it gave a lot of employment at that time.

Scoraiochting, visiting the neighbours, exchanging news and gossip and card playing was another social activity of the time in the house. The old people were great at telling stories, any children listening would be afraid to go to bed if the topic was ghostly in case they would see the fairies or ghosts.

Water was drawn from a spring well, which was close to the dwelling house, there was also a barrel under every eave chute in the yard to catch the rain water, this was used in the house for washing clothes and general

cleaning inside and outside, and was also given to the animals and poultry. Clothes were hand washed in bath tubs using soap as a detergent, the
clothes were then hung out on a line or put on the bushes to dry.

The iron for ironing the clothes at that time was the same shape as
today's, only a triangular piece of iron would be put into a red fire, when
hot it was put into the open end and closed in, then it was ready. Also that
time the men's collars especially the grandfathers, would be starched
before ironing. All the cooking and baking was done on an open fire, food
was either boiled, stewed or roasted in pot hanging from a crook over the
fire. Bread was baked in a bastible, dough placed in a hot bastible and hung
over a hot fire. Coal and turf was placed on the lid of the bastible to provide an even heat all round just like the oven of today.

In the winter the women knitted socks and jumpers, an extra few sets of
knitting needles and wool would be in readiness for any woman who came
to visit, and they would join in as well. Women made a lot of quilts with
material, crochet, patchwork and embroidery. They made some lovely crochet bedspreads, shawls, mass clothes, table cloths, pillow covers, cushion

*Jim Dwyer, Marie Cronin & Mick Burke with mowing machine
in Munigave in 1940s.*

covers and christening robes. The older women wore hooded cloaks called 'West Cork Cloaks'. The local tailor made the men's suits. a dressmaker made the women's dresses, skirts, blouses and coats. Most of the babies were born at home with a dedicated midwife as well as the local doctor present. Babies were christened the day after they were born, not like today when they could be christened three months later. There was a hospital in Dunmanway, but this was only for taking care of the sick people.

All old people in their last years when not able to look after themselves where cared for in their own homes by one of their family. Care would be shared among the family members. When the person died, they would be laid out in their beds wearing a brown shroud, waked at home for a night or two, and then taken to a church for mass before burial in Kinneigh, Kilmichael, or what ever parish they belonged to.

The only traffic on the roads was the horse and cart, donkeys were also used. The wheels of the cart were made of timber with steel binding. This was done in the forge by the blacksmith. He made shoes and shod the horses and iron implements too. This was a great place for chatting, and often children called in on the way home from school to see him work the hot iron. People travelled to mass on ponies and traps, while others walked, rode the bicycle, or later on, by motor car.

The local shops were Daly's Gloun and Pake Murphy's, later known as Ted and Pat McCarthy's in Coppeen, where the neighbours did their grocery shopping and collected some feed stuff for the animals and poultry. The got their grain ground in the mill in the fifties. Money was scarce but an old pound would buy a lot. I remember the price of the *Cork Examiner* was 2 pence.

Ration books were issued in the war years 1940–1950 for tea, sugar, flour, bread, butter and wheat meal, one would register with your shopkeeper and he would take the coupons from the book as you do your shopping.

The harness maker was the man to make and repair the tackling for horses. The shoemaker made and repaired the shoes for the families. Mr. Heb Shorten of Coppeen repaired many an eight-day clock and watch.

Cillíns

Cillins are burial grounds, usually of unbaptised children. The ground they cover is unconsecrated and not usually associated with a church. The practice of burying unbaptised babies in Cillíns continued into the early decades of the twentieth century. As these children had died before being baptised the Church would not allow them to be buried in consecrated church graveyards. Not only babies were buried here it seems, sometimes unidentified bodies found in the parish and suicide victims were also buried here.

These burial places occur all over the countryside, usually in locations that are seen as liminal, the state of being 'in-between', on the margins. Apparently the Latin word límen means on the threshold. The souls of the dead buried in a Cillin were spiritually condemned to Limbo, disallowed into consecrated ground. So too were the bodies, physically condemned to life on the margins, on the threshold. These Cillins occur at road sides, at cross roads, by rivers and streams, in the corner of fields, on the edge of townlands, on clifftops. Sometimes ringforts were used or a site with Early Christian associations. The word Cillin contains another Latin word, Cill. This word often occurs in names of places that had or may have had an association with an Early Christian cell church, where monks would have lived a life of contemplation away from the main monastic and religious centres.

Placenames are associated with some of these burial grounds, names like Croisín na Leanabh. Sometime these graves were marked with lumps of quartz stone or the quartz could also be placed directly on the coffin or body. Some known local Cillíns are in Belrose Upper, Kilnacranagh (Parknakilla) and Lissarourke.

Castletown Kinneigh

The Village of Castletown Kinneigh in which Dan McCarthy grew up was an industrious, self-sufficient bustling community. There were a number of trade businesses located in the village. These included two blacksmiths (including Thade Crowley), four masons, two carpenters, two tailors and a tinsmith (O'Driscolls) The blacksmiths worked from 8am to 10pm. There were apprentices assigned to most trades. One postman served the area.

The public house was to have been in what is now Moore's family home. Instead a license was granted to the Harrington family who built premises on ground that had belonged to Hosfords. It was sold in 1915–16 to sisters named Nyhan, one of whom married an O'Callaghan. There were four shops in the village: (1) Jeremiah O'Mahony's (the author, historian, teacher, and father of Rev. Liam O'Mahony. O'Mahonys shop was also the Post Office); (2) Johanna McCarthy's (where Dan McCarthy lived); (3) Nyhans – later O'Callaghans, also a public house; and (4) Moores.

Castletown Church was built in the 1870s and replaced an older church which was located just to the left of the present building. The entrance to the old church is marked by a cross on the wall on the roadside. Most of the money for the building of the new church was donated by former residents of the area who had emigrated to America.

Farming: Hay was cut by six to seven men using scythes. Turf was cut at Farranmareen bog. There were many farm labourers resident in the village area. Ten men worked on Hosfords farm.

The following names are associated with the Céim Road: Bob Kiely, Creedon, and Jack Ryan who was a caretaker for Lord Bandon, and Coughlans. From the latter family came the illustrious Colonel Coughlan. In old dwellings it was a common practice to knock chimneys to avoid paying rent.

Castletown National School: There was a boys' and a girls' school which was preceded by an older school. In charge of the boys' school was a master with a lady assistant. Two ladies were in charge of the girls' school. Dan McCarthy first began school in 1914.

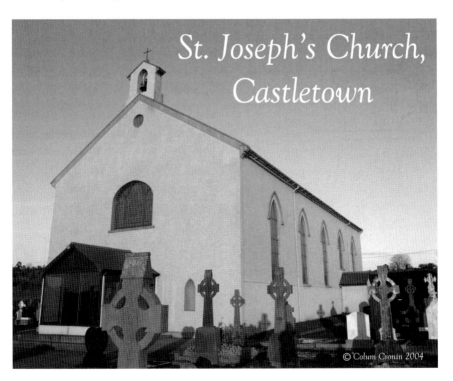

St. Joseph's Church, Castletown

© Colum Cronin 2004

There was strict segregation of the sexes. Under British rule, little Irish history was taught. The emphasis seemed to be on places around the world where British troops were stationed. However, with the coming of the Free State, there seemed to be an increased emphasis on Irish language, to the exclusion of other subjects. Dan himself learned Irish from his grandparents.

Colonel Coughlan built a house at Port a Locha where he resided for seven years. The creamery which stood at the spot now known as 'the creamery cross' closed in 1925.

Sports meetings in the village were at that time organised by Sinn Fein. There was a Harrier Club which broke up in 1925. The present club was formed in 1954.

Colonel Coughlan produced the first electricity in Castletown Kinneigh. This electricity was produced by a water wheel which was located south of Dullea's gate. He had earlier built such a wheel for Conner's of Manch. The project in Castletown was begun in August 1942 and the light was switched on in December 8th of that same year.

Dan McCarthy worked for Cork County Council for 33 years. His area included West Cork as far as Bantry.

According to Bruno O'Donoghue, in 1831 there were fifty seven houses in the village. McCarthy castle stood near the 'town' off the Céim road. This castle, along with the town were burned by Cromwellian soldiers in 1651. A large paper factory was located south of the village. There were three public houses, four shops, 3 carpenters, 2 tailors, 3 stone masons, 2 thatchers, 2 tinsmiths, 3 dressmakers, a hood cloak maker, 2 midwives, and a cattle jobber, all resident in Castletown in pre-famine times.

My Local Area

The school in Coppeen was built in 1931. It used to be on the corner near the main road. Just outside the village, there is a fort called Cahirvagliair Ringfort. It was restored in 1983–84. Local folklore says that Brian Boru was held hostage here between the ages of 8 and 16.

The clubs in the area include Diarmuid Ó Mathúna's GAA Club, Castletown Table Tennis, Autograss, Soccer, Ladies' Club, Bowling, Harriers, IFA, Coppeen A.H.C.S, Community Alert, Coppeen Coursing Club, Céilí Classes, Weight Lifting, Coppeen National School, Play School and Coppeen Golfing Society. The church in Castletown is called St. Joseph's.

The school in Coppeen is called Coppeen National School. It has an average of 10 pupils in each class. It was built in 1931. It has three main teachers and two resource teachers.

For such a small village, it has a mill, a shop, a post office, a Ready Mix Plant, a grotto, a pub and a terrace. There is a giants grave in Slieveowen, just above Coppeen. On his grave stone there are his fingerprints. Coppeen is a lovely place to live in. There is no church in Coppeen but there is in Castletown. One of the main cottage industries of Coppeen in former times was that of poitín. Truth be told, people travelled far and wide to purchase and taste this illegal alcohol. Many people still recall a story of the journey they had to make to buy this product. If caught people received big fines and their stills were destroyed. However this did not dampen their enthusiasm of establishing a new still and trying again. One time they were moving a large amount of poitín in a milk tank and the guards were given a tip off about it. So half an hour later before the move happened there was a report went in to the garda station that a body was found floating on the nearby river, so all the detectives and gardaí went to investigate that … meanwhile the bulk tank of poitín passed off happily and safely along the road. And not to be dwelling too much on alcohol but … for a while an ambulance was used to transport the poitín and in all fairness this was a genius plan because no check point would hold up a rushing ambulance.

To finish with I must talk about St. Patrick's Day The participants in the parade, including bands from all over the country used to march twice around the village centre. The parade was very popular and brought people from far and near. Although the weather was (and still is 36 years later) generally very cold, it was an opportunity to come together and meet the neighbours. The parade was featured several times on RTÉ News, so Coppeen had its 15 minutes of fame.

By Stephanie Hayes, Coppeen National School

The 35 Scamps of Coppeen

A goat drive was held on a cold stormy night
I came there myself to see the great sight.
The game was played squarely, the goat in full view.
While the fiddle was tuned by our Bold Donoghue.

There were tinkers and tailors, soldiers and waivers,
Mick Fehily the mason was stuck in between.
We had Sheila and Sean and the rakes of Fidaún
And the 35 scamps now that came from Coppeen.

John the Captain came first and Curtin as well
Says the Captain to Curtin; tonight we'll have hell
I was told at my dinner by a man very keen
There were 35 scamps on the road from Coppeen

Curtin stood up and took out a pound note
Take your bob out of that till I play the auld goat
Hurry up with the game we don't want to be seen,
They would steal our small change, the scamps of Coppeen

Four couples sat down then for to play
Says the captain to Larry, 'tis coming our way
This man stood up with this scarf round his throat
Saying Larry auld boy we're 25 for the goat

The game was squared over when the scamps arrived in
They looked for refreshments, there was nothing within
Pay up says Larry, and join in the fun
And we called poor old Seanin for Woods's to run.

They sent Sean to Rebecca for 10 pair of bread
Says Larry to Hannah those men must be fed
An invitation to Alfred we don't want to be mean
And not to open his mouth about the scamps of Coppeen

Alfred came down and his jaw was so long,
He said to Jim Warren we can't stay very long,
Tell that girl come out and don't let her be seen
For they'll tell Rebecca, the scamps of Coppeen.

I came there myself t'was late in the night
The news that I have gave me a great fright
The bread was all stolen, the jams and the cream
T'was ate on the road by the scamps of Coppeen

I met Larry next morning, he looked pale and white
'O gracious' said he 'we had a tearing old night'
While water will run, and grasses grow green
We will ne'er play our goat for the boy's of Coppeen

Maggie Long was the winner, oh she had the luck
And now she's the owner of a fine premium buck
He stands here in Clash, a prince to be seen
Let ye all bring your goats here, ye scamps of Coppeen

Excuse my poor rhyme, its not very keen,
My name is John Dave, I hail from Coppeen
I am an art teacher, and plain to be seen
For to educate my pupils, the scamps of Coppeen

Scoraiocht in Coppeen on 5th Sept. 2004

Acknowledgements

Many people have helped us during this project and we extend our thanks to each one of you.

Síle, Liam and Joan Murphy, Willie Hurley, Noirín Hurley, Sam Kingston, John Noel Murphy, Pat Murphy, Stephanie Larkin, Val Wood, Con and Theresa O'Driscoll, Michael Galvin, Denis Murphy, Mary Morgan, Antoinette O'Donovan, Mim O'Donovan, Margaret Walsh, Don Wood, Seamus Crowley, Den Lordan, Margaret Hurley, Richard Sweetnam, Thomas Riedmuller, Mary Cross, Patrick Kelleher, Denis Carroll, Angela Forde, Breda Crowley, Michael O'Donovan, Shane Cronin, Nan O'Donovan, Sean Hurley, Marie Cohalan, Eamon Galvin, Nuala Lordan, Rose Cronin, Margaret Moloney, Gerard Lordan, Ned Barrett, Feenie O'Driscoll, Sean and Julia O'Mahony, Donal Kelly, Berni Whyte, Nora Cremin, Johnny Long, Theresa Barrett, Rev. Judith Hubbard-Jones, Kate Dwyer, Denis O'Mahony.

Special thanks to:
Stephanie Larkin and Rita O'Neill for proof reading.
Michael Crowley for his many words of wisdom.
Denis Cronin for his endless days of effort.
The teachers and pupils of Coppeen National School.
Therése and Conor Bourke, proprietors of 'An Caipín' for their ongoing kindness and hospitality.

Thanks especially to all the members of CAHCS who helped in bringing this project to fruition, not least the working committee who met regularly and kept up the momentum.

If we have omitted anybody it has not been deliberate, as everybody's contribution has been most gratefully appreciated.

CAHCS Website: www.coppeenheritage.com

CAHCS Email: info@coppeenheritage.com

Bibliography

Creedon, C. ,The Cork, *Bandon and South Coast Railway Vol. 1 – An Illustrated History*.

Cronin, C., 'The Fair of Ballabuidhe' from the album *Peace in the Harbour* (1985).

Galvin, M. *Pure Pride – Mid Cork* (1904).

Manning, C., *The Journal of Irish Archaeology* IV 87/8.

O'Brien, W., *Sacred Ground: Megalithic Tombs in Costal Southwest Ireland*, National University of Ireland, Galway, Department of Archaeology (1999).

O'Donoghue, B., *Parish Histories and Place Names of West Cork* (1961).

O'Keeffe, T., *Ireland's Round Towers, Buildings, Rituals and Landscapes of the Early Irish Church*, Stroud, Tempus Publishing Ltd (2004).

O'Mahony, J., *West Cork and Its Story*. Tower Books Cork (1961)

The Southern Star newspaper.